Praise for How...

I am using this book in a class that I am teaching; it is one of the best books on the subject of the Law of Attraction. A must read. *Loretta Brooks, Centers for Spiritual Living, New York City.*

I bought this book about two months ago and it is life changing. I am practicing the simple easy to follow lessons on how to activate the Law of Attraction that she has in this book, every day. Love, love, love this book. *RM*

I am a Law of Attraction junkie and have read nearly everything out there. This is definitely the best book out there on the Law of Attraction. I Love Abraham-Hicks and the Seth books as well, but it wasn't until I read *How to Allow* that I really Got It! Somehow this book has a certain magic to it that explains things so clearly and creates a sense of hopefulness that I can do this. It has been a life changer for me. I can't say strongly enough that everyone should read this book. *KC*

Just after finishing *How to Allow,* I had a recent open house (I'm a Realtor) with 40 people, which is nothing short of amazing, tons of showings on a new listing in a buyers' market, movement with an elderly client who's reluctant to move but needs to, and . . . best of all, a telephone call from someone I care about deeply for the first time in 30 years!!! My goal is to focus on what I want, remember that it's ok to be selfish and expect the best, and let the Universe work out the timing and details. *NJ*

I was introduced to the Law of Attraction a couple of years ago by a friend. I had never heard of it, but immediately recognized that I had already been living my life according to many of the principles, as things always seemed to go my way. To enhance my positive connection with the Universe, I purchased the movie, "The Secret," and followed that up with the book "The Power." These gave a good description of the Law of Attraction and many uses for it, but for me, seemed impersonal and played to those who were just learning about the law. Last summer I was looking for a book that would remind me what I needed to do to get back on track if I veered a little, and came across *How to Allow* by Susan Shearer Young. It immediately became my favorite book, which I read every couple of months. I can read it all the way through in about three hours, and it puts my "vibration level" right where I want it to be. Susan teaches how to allow yourself to align with the Universe, which is what needs to occur for good things to happen in your life. We all have a connection with the Universe, but she shows how to make it positive, and do it on purpose. Her book contains real-life examples of the power of the Universe at work, and provides tools to raise and maintain your level of vibration. One of the things that Susan stresses is to make happiness our highest goal. When we're happy, we naturally have an elevated vibration, and positively affect those around us. I keep that in mind every day, and use the simple tools Susan lays out to keep me on track. This is by far the best book I've come across on the subject, and will continue to go back to it. *JG*

I discovered Susan's book just recently. I felt as if she had taken me by the hand, served me a soothing tea and with such gentleness helped me further understand the Law of Attraction. I practiced what she had suggested and got immediate results. My life is reflecting that practice! It was just the information I needed to move me forward. Reading her words has taught me also how important it is to introduce new ideas and concepts in a gentle and kind and user-friendly manner. This is a perfect gift for any level of understanding, beginner or advanced. *TM*

Thank you Susan Shearer Young and your wonderful book, *How to Allow*. It helped me in ways I never imagined. Forever grateful and I feel I met you for a reason. *SB*

I loved this book on the Law of Attraction and the Art of Allowing. As a busy working mom, I found this book easy to read, even when I was super tired from work and wearing my "mommy hat." The examples Susan gives are easy to understand and apply in my life. I continue to reread this book because the Law of

Attraction does work—and Susan, through her book, tells you how to easily manifest the life you really want! If you want to live the life you are dreaming of, buy this book! *CW*

Sincerely, Susan Young's book *How to Allow* is more than a book, it's also a well-planned, EFFECTIVE course and the e-book is definitely the best $29 investment I have ever made. I experienced a major shift in perspective right at the start of her book. Not long after, many opportunities started coming my way, quite unexpectedly. I was named for and then interviewed for a promotion and was awarded it. At first I thought the promotion would be for approximately $3,000, possibly twice a year. It turned out to be a promotion for $5,000 that fall—(they asked me if $5,000 was okay), and another $5,000 in the spring. I was shocked when I found out they needed me in the summer too. You guessed it, another $5,000. Beginning the next school year, they extended an offer to continue and offered me a raise for $13,500 for both semesters. (This is in addition to my regular salary). In addition to these opportunities, private clients have been coming my way for help with personal statements for graduate school or editing an art auction catalogue. These clients have been higher caliber than previous ones and a pleasure to work with ... I know my value and I'm communicating that better. The investment in Susan's book and course was well worth it, many times over. Thank you Susan, for showing us *How to Allow*. I will keep revisiting the course for inspiration. *DH*

I just devoured *How to Allow* in one day, and I believe your book is one of the best bar none. You made the concepts easy to understand and implement. I really enjoy using the Daily Tune-up because it helps me raise my vibration easily. What a concept: make feeling good your main objective and the rest will take care of itself. *KY*

One of the best, most compelling, useful books I have ever read. Susan Shearer Young is awesome in her presentation. A practical guide that should be must reading for everyone who wants to take control of their own destiny. *LM*

I 'love' this book! With myriad Law of Attraction books and processes to choose from, a feeling of overwhelm is the state many, if not most, conscious creators operate from . . . and I've often been among them, wondering if I'm really doing enough. Susan Young understands what an impediment this frustrating vibrational undercurrent is, and has outlined a smart, simple, and very effective system that not only ensures that we 'are' doing enough, but also helps us to 'feel' that we are. Personally, I've found this system super-effective as well as simple to institute and so enjoyable to incorporate into my daily life. *BP*

This book is AWESOME, by the way—really, really good! And, fyi, I read a lot of LOA books. *BL*

I want to tell you that *How to Allow* is really making a difference. Not long after I purchased it, I also purchased some CD programs by Abraham-Hicks. I really did not consciously know how the overlap would be so empowering. For years, I've been a believer in the Law of Attraction. I now understand two more laws—The Law of Deliberate Creation and the Art of Allowing. You book has helped me so much with regard to allowing. I did not understand the long-programmed resistances inside me. I'm still dealing with them, but much more productively now. Again, thank you; and bless you. *DJ*

Love Susan Shearer Young's book! I had read other Law of Attraction books and had even attended some workshops. This book gave me the tools I needed to consistently create the life I always dreamed of. Everything is different; my finances improved, relationships evolved, and new people and opportunities started showing up in my life effortlessly! Susan has a unique gift as a writer. She is able to take complex, esoteric ideas and break them down into easy and practical steps. *DG*

Excellent read for learning how to apply the Law of Attraction. Simple and clear exercises that systematically guide you to creating the reality you desire. I am already experiencing the positive changes I put forth in my life. If you follow the work of Abraham, you will embrace this book with joy. *SB*

Finished the e-book. I'm actually re-reading it. I felt your e-book was very well written. Much easier to do a "method" of daily activities to "allow more." I ordered a few of the books you suggested at the back, to continue on, but your way of explaining and "doing" is the best I have encountered so far. I never had too much luck on the visualization and feelings of euphoria I was told to conjure up in some of the other books. *JS*

I'm still not finished with the book (very close though). I've been trying to really let everything sink in as much as possible. I've noticed little things happening but today was the first day that I KNEW that your process works. About a year and a half ago, I got into some legal trouble and had to hire a lawyer. The stress of paying my lawyer on top of other court costs has had me extremely stressed out. Today, my lawyer's paralegal called from out of nowhere. Instead of panicking like I normally do, I said to myself. . . . "The reason she's calling is good and positive." Sure enough, out of the blue, she said that my lawyer had authorized her to reduce my fees by $500. I asked her why he had agreed to do this and her response was, "Because he likes you"! I just want to thank you for helping me get on the track of allowing. You truly are a blessing in my life right now! *HW*

. . . . . Started reading your book and started understanding exactly how to put my desires out there! To the Universe . . . way cool . . .I am now dating a very gentle, smart, caring person, just the way I had hoped for . . . And that, only time will tell, but so far the "best" match for the desires of the heart! So it really works and, I am, will encourage anyone to combine the movie (The Secret) and your book to get a full understanding of what is bigger than all of us. I am not religious, but here is something that does not have to involve a church or a place of worship, it's simply all around us, to use all the time, it really makes me smile, just the thought of it! Thank you for writing this book Susan, it has changed my life, and I will better the lives of others by sharing all of what I have learned. *CV*

I just wanted to say a very sincere thank you to you. I purchased your e-book and the corresponding audio and find that you really have something fresh and unique to offer. I love the journaling with the prompts that you gave, and feel a real change. I was suffering from consuming book after book on this topic and other similar topics . . . but I was never doing anything concrete to put ideas into action. You have given me an amazing rest from the constant reading. Now I feel I am doing. Thanks again, and I hope many good things come your way. *EW*

I bought your e-book *How to Allow* and it's simply amazing. It was just extremely soothing and gives a new trust and faith that well-being is coming. I probably bought it more than a month back, but I keep going back to it and it's great to keep reading. There are a lot of small things that I keep attracting and other signs that keep nudging me, giving me intuition that the path I am following to keep going towards better feeling thoughts, etc. is the right one. Thanks for everything. *CL*

I cannot say enough great things about *How to Allow*. I purchased this book about a year ago and have been floored at times with how much my life has improved since. Susan created an easy to use system that takes the guesswork out of deliberate creation. I started researching the Law of Attraction a few years ago and although I believed it worked, my results were somewhat inconsistent and spotty. Thankfully, *How to Allow* filled in the missing pieces and has taught me the skills I was lacking for effective creation. Her book is THE manual you need to really put the Law of Attraction into action. It's simple and easy to understand and most importantly, it works! I'm forever grateful for this well written insightful and life altering book! *LM*

How to Allow

Working with the Law of Attraction to Allow Your Natural Well-Being

How to Allow

A Simple System for Energy Alignment

Both the writer and publisher have prepared this book/course to the best of their abilities but make no representation as to the accuracy, applicability, or completeness of this book. They disclaim any warranties (express or implied), merchantability or appropriateness for a specific purpose. Please seek the advice of a competent professional. All references are for informational purposes only and are not warranted for content, accuracy or any other implied or explicit purpose. This book/course contains material protected under International and Federal Copyright Laws.

The names and identifying details of certain persons have been changed to protect their privacy.

Copyright © 2017 by Susan Shearer Young
The Book is the exclusive property of: Susan Shearer Young

Original Cover Art by SCA Svenska Cellulosa Aktiebolagot

For Kendall, Duncan and Parker

You continue to be my inspiration to be my best self.

TABLE OF CONTENTS

REVISED AND UPDATED INTRODUCTION	1
INTRODUCTION	6
WHY THIS COURSE WAS CREATED	12
HOW THIS COURSE CAME ABOUT	15
LAW OF ATTRACTION AND ALLOWING—THE BASIC PRINCIPLES	20
UNDERSTANDING THE CONCEPT OF ALLOWING	25
BEING AWARE OF YOUR VIBRATION - YOUR EMOTIONAL GUIDANCE SYSTEM	27
INTRODUCTION TO THE SYSTEM—THE DAILY TOOLS	33
LESSON ONE: MAKING ONE DECISION	34
LESSON TWO: SETTING YOUR INTENTIONS	46
LESSON THREE: LAYING YOUR FOUNDATION - MAKING PEACE WITH WHERE YOU ARE	58
LESSON FOUR: THE FIRST DAILY TOOL - TUNING UP YOUR VIBRATION	73
HOW THE PROCESS FOR TUNING UP YOUR VIBRATION WORKS	82
UNDERSTANDING THE GOAL OF THE TUNING UP PROCESS	87
TUNING UP YOUR VIBRATION—THE PROCESS!!	90
LESSON FIVE: THE SECOND DAILY TOOL - GOING WITHIN AND RELEASING RESISTANCE	119
LESSON SIX: ANY BLOCKS? - RELEASING FALSE BELIEFS	130
LESSON SEVEN: ALLOWING IMPROVED RELATIONSHIPS	150
LESSON EIGHT: HELPFUL TIPS FOR STAYING ON TRACK	160
LESSON NINE: INSPIRED ACTION - LIVING LIFE IN THE FIELD OF APPRECIATION	170
RECOMMENDED RESOURCES	179

Revised and Updated Introduction

When I sat down to begin writing *How to Allow*, I was filled with a sense of purpose, an overwhelming desire to share what I had learned about the Law of Attraction. I had known about the Law of Attraction for years; I was absolutely certain that I was creating my own reality with my thoughts. The whole concept of God and Universal Energy now made complete sense to me. It was such a relief to learn that we had been given the freedom to choose whatever we wanted in life, that nothing is being imposed upon us.

Although I was quickly reminded of that famous wisdom, "with great freedom comes great responsibility." In this case, the freedom to choose exactly what we want in our lives had a bit of a Catch-22, or what seemed to me at the time to be a similar hurdle. While we live in a world where absolute Well-Being is intended to be the norm for us, and we have the ability to be, or do or have whatever we desire, we have to generate a vibration that matches our desires, the good feelings of already having what we want, before we can allow what we want into our lives. That purposeful creation of feelings matching the high vibration of our desires is what is known as "Allowing Your Natural Well-Being."

When I learned this important piece of information about the Law of Attraction, I just did not find it easy to consistently get myself into those good feeling vibrations that matched my desires before I had actually received the desires in my physical reality. It was to be an ongoing lesson, one at which I have become better and better. But, once you know this important information and are able to prove to yourself that you can create what you want, it can become very easy to be judgmental about yourself and your efforts. When things aren't going the way you want, it can become far too easy to feel discouraged, as if you just aren't good at deliberate creation, that you just can't manage your own vibration, that is, the thoughts and accompanying emotions you are feeling. I knew that I could find a way to get better at this and create more of the things I wanted in my life.

    I received incredible intuitive guidance, which nearly knocked me over, that I was to write a book that provided a system of simple rituals that people could follow so that they would really understand how the Law of Attraction works and, most importantly, see the evidence of their efforts for themselves. This evidence would allow people to know that they could be good at deliberate creation. And, it would only get better from there. I knew that these rituals worked for me; I had stopped feeling like I was a sloppy creator (most of the time), and knew that this simple approach could help others to finally get a real handle on working with the Law of Attraction.

    I imagined this book, of course, and felt the feeling of having created this book, before I brought it into being. Otherwise this book would not exist. That's just the way the Laws of the Universe work. I imagined people buying this book and benefitting from this book because that is exactly what I desired. When I completed this book, I knew that in order for it to reach other people looking for this information, I needed to love my book, to believe it was the amazingly helpful guide that it was intended to be. And, as I re-read my book, I felt that incredible feeling that this book *is* really great. It *is* going to help lots of people. It really *is* the best book, or one of the best books, out there right now on the Law of Attraction. It's one of the few to focus on the Allowing part of the equation, which is really the only part of the process that is our work if we want to create the lives we want.

What I didn't imagine in exact form, but what resulted from this visualizing and imagining, was lots and lots of people writing to me and telling me that *How to Allow* had literally changed their lives for the better in some amazing ways. Even some Law of Attraction experts told me that they finally "got it" after reading this book, in a way they had never understood it before. One person contacted me to tell me that she wanted me to know that my book had saved the mother of two young children, as she had been so discouraged that she had considered taking "lots of pills" prior to listening to *How to Allow* on audio. She said the book had given her hope that happiness was possible. That was very unexpected and continues to be something I will never forget.

A prominent radio host told me, "You are so smart; you are the first person to be able to take all of that complex information and make it easy to understand." She said she had finally really "gotten the Law of Attraction" for the first time. So that Harvard Law degree that was languishing while I was absorbed with this journey wasn't a wasted effort. All of that work to become more analytical was helpful in taking esoteric concepts and revealing them in a way that was easy to apply. It was all very gratifying to hear.

What I also had not visualized exactly, other than within the emotion of loving my book, was that *How to Allow* would win the award for "Best of Books on Law of Attraction for 2012." I could not have imagined winning that award, as I hadn't known that it existed. It was wonderful to see that my efforts were being appreciated and that people were benefitting so much from my attempt to pass on what I had learned through my life experiences. Although the outcome of winning the award felt fantastic, I'm not sure that I didn't feel even more fantastic about seeing that my visualizing and focusing upon my book as "the best or, one of the best, books out there on the Law of Attraction" had worked so perfectly to create a book judged as Best of Books on Law of Attraction. How could there be a better example of how these principles really work? And, I continue to learn more about how the laws work every day and know that it can get better and better and better.

Although *How to Allow* was originally published as an e-book, a Kindle, Nook and Apple book, among others, and then an audio book, many people have asked for a copy of the book that they could hold in their hands. Some have asked for an autographed copy, which was impossible to pull off with an e-book. So, while *How to Allow* has helped so many and continues to help more people "get it" in it's current form, I received my marching orders from above to create an updated print version for those who are looking for and attracting that into their lives.

So, a huge thank you to the many, many people who have related their successes and improvements in their lives after reading this book. You have made me feel as if every bit of effort, which has been mostly a complete pleasure, has been worthwhile. Thank you for helping me to create exactly what I wanted to manifest into my life. I can't wait for the next chapter.

Susan Shearer Young

Introduction

Welcome to this book and course I've entitled *How to Allow*. If you've been attracted to this course, it's likely that you're already familiar with the Law of Attraction, although you may or may not be familiar with the concept of ***Allowing* your Well-Being**. It's not essential, however, that you have any prior knowledge of either the Law of Attraction or the concept of Allowing in order to reap incredible benefits from this course.

This course is designed both for those who are already trying to work with the Law of Attraction to become better deliberate creators and for those who are new to the concept and looking to create a better quality of life. It's my intention that you find this to be one of the most practical guides to working with both the Law of Attraction and the concept of Allowing which is available anywhere, and that you'll go on to create what will seem like miracles in your life!

When we begin the substance of this course, I'll provide plenty of information on both the Law of Attraction and Allowing and how they operate to create your experiences, in order to make sure that we are all operating from the same information when we begin to apply the powerful tools used in this course.

For those with little or no knowledge of the Law of Attraction, however, I'd like to explain very briefly that it is a universal law that states that energy attracts like energy. As scientists are confirming that everything in our Universe is made of energy that vibrates, many people are coming to understand that our thoughts are also made of energy and that those thoughts carry their own vibration. These vibrations we create with our thoughts draw into our lives other thoughts, circumstances and people with similarly vibrating energy. The Law of Attraction, therefore, explains how we attract our own experiences and circumstances by the thoughts we think. This explains the phrase, "You get what you think about."

The counterpart of the Law of Attraction, the notion of Allowing, refers to the concept of letting yourself connect with your own natural Well-Being or the Infinite Intelligence of the Universe while working with the Law of Attraction. Connecting with this Infinite Intelligence is known as *Allowing* because it is based on the premise that there is a dominant stream of Well-Being in our Universe, which we can either Allow ourselves to connect with or resist.

It is the act of Allowing ourselves to connect with this stream of Well-Being that is really our role in managing the process of attracting the things we want into our lives. It is how we attract on purpose, rather than attracting whatever matches our vibration, wanted or unwanted. And, it is this notion of Allowing our connection to the Infinite Intelligence of the Universe so that we can create the lives we want that is the focus of this course.

What kinds of things will you learn in this course to help you to Allow yourself to connect with the Infinite Intelligence of the Universe?

You'll learn to raise your vibration to a consistently higher level through the use of two simple daily rituals. You will actually raise your vibrational set point, the frequency you gravitate toward regularly.

You'll learn tools to help maintain your vibration throughout the day or when faced with challenging circumstances.

You'll learn to be aware of where you're vibrating and how to ramp up your vibration before undertaking tasks in your day, so that you'll have the outcome you're hoping for more often.

You'll also learn how to pay less attention to, and sometimes to ignore, your "reality" (if there's room for improvement) and to focus upon your desires so that they become your new reality.

And, what kinds of things can you expect to happen in your life when you Allow yourself to connect with Infinite Intelligence on a regular basis? Although this course will be filled with practical examples, I'll mention some of the results I've seen when people begin managing their vibration on purpose. When you make raising your vibration a top priority, you engage the resources of Infinite Intelligence, which go to work to fulfill your desires. Infinite Intelligence or Source

Energy brings together a cast of thousands to line up people, circumstances and events, which combine to deliver just what you've asked for. In my own life and that of my family, friends, and people I've counseled, I've seen miraculous results:

- Relationships that seemed beyond repair were mended.

- Illnesses have been healed.

- Money has arrived from unexpected sources.

- Long-awaited partners have been attracted.

- Objects and resources have materialized.

- Other family members have begun to thrive.

- Guidance has been received.

- "Coincidences" providing contacts, resources, or information have occurred.

- Small "everyday" miracles happen often.

Frequently, things happen quickly and almost effortlessly when you make maintaining your vibration your top priority. Sometimes, the new things you begin to attract can be life changing and sometimes they just make each day more fun. In a perfect everyday example of Allowing my natural Well-Being, I recently received a gift I wanted but had never even asked for. You will learn how the Universe hears your requests even if they are not formally spoken. These types of "coincidences" happen often when you work at raising your vibration.

I was standing in the family room of our new home and random thoughts were going through my mind: "We could use a new magazine rack in this room. The magazines are really piling up on the coffee table. Didn't we have a magazine rack in our old house? What we could use in this room is a dark wood, more finished looking, magazine rack. And, it would need to be large because this room is on a pretty large scale. Hmmmm. That would be nice."

I continued to straighten up the room and didn't give it a second thought. I didn't write it down as a goal or say a prayer to God or to the Universe. I just thought, "That would be nice." The very next day, my mother-in-law called to discuss our plans for the holidays when she'd be driving up to visit. She asked if we could use an antique magazine rack that she was no longer using. She mentioned that it was large, mahogany, had belonged to her grandmother, and she wasn't using it in her new home. Could she bring it to us when she came up for

Christmas? All I could think was, "Wow!" And, of course, "Thanks."

Now, that perfect gift at the perfect time wasn't exactly life changing, but is a perfect example of how we can attract the things we want into our lives when we take the time to tune up our vibration to connect with our natural Well-Being. You can attract small things or life-changing windfalls. The same principles apply equally to creating a free parking space or attracting millions of dollars. When you tune up your vibration, you naturally attract people who treat you well, improve your health, finances, and well, virtually anything that you decide to focus upon. It's simply the way the laws work. You get what matches your vibration.

This course will be filled with stories of small victories as well as life-changing creations, which will provide practical examples of Allowing in action so that you can see easily how the tools might be applied in your own life. Before we go further, however, I'd like to give you some brief background on how this course was created so that you have some understanding of how I arrived at this point in my understanding and my intentions for this course.

Why This Course Was Created

While there is much information that has become available on the Law of Attraction, particularly since the release of the movie, "The Secret," many people have found it difficult to create the results they want, particularly without understanding the concept of Allowing. This course seeks to provide a bridge to harnessing the Law of Attraction more consciously by explaining the all-important step of Allowing and providing tools for Allowing that are both easy to grasp and apply.

This course takes a uniquely practical approach to working with the Law of Attraction; it is unique in that it is a results-oriented *system*, a program with simple Daily Tools that work to create more consistent results by helping you to raise and maintain your vibration.

When I was listening to my own inner guidance as I felt the inspiration for developing this course, I looked up to see a sign directly in front of me that said,

The System is the Solution.

I could not have put it better! As humans, we thrive on ritual and our repeated patterns of behavior. Most of the successes we achieve in life are based on rituals developed over time, which have become second nature to us. Inconsistent, scattered efforts often fail because they don't re-program the thinking on which they are based. Because this program is simple to use as a daily ritual, it provides a solution to the spotty results achieved by most people who use a variety of Law of Attraction or manifesting techniques on an inconsistent basis. These daily rituals help us to literally change our thought patterns to ones that are in vibrational harmony with all of the things we'd like to bring into our lives.

If you use the two Daily Tools set forth in the course, you should begin to see almost immediate, positive changes in the circumstances of your life. If you'd like to take charge of your experiences and live the incredible life you were meant to live, it's time to start playing the game of life consciously using the Laws of the Universe. These laws, like the law of gravity, never waiver, and if you follow the program, it is not only possible, but inevitable, that you'll fulfill many of your fondest desires!

I know that, in many cases, it may be perfectly acceptable to flip through a course and find those parts that resonate with you and work with them in any particular order. That really is not the case for this course! I will introduce two important Daily Tools in Lessons Four and Five, which are the cornerstones of this course, but it is essential that you go through the exercises in the first three lessons that precede the Daily Tools in order to lay the proper foundation.

> *In fact, the application of the first three lessons will actually help you to attract support from the Universe for using the Daily Tools more effectively.*

You will see, that as everything relating to raising your vibration is a mental game, it's vitally important to understand exactly the sort of attitude and feeling you're trying to create and why, before you are able to apply the Daily Tools effectively. And, the first three lessons help to lay that important foundation that will put you in the proper frame of mind for using the Daily Tools.

How This Course Came About

Nearly fifteen years ago, as I was trying to learn to meditate, I received an internal wake-up call from a voice within, which clearly wasn't my own. I was asking the question, "Who am I and why am I here?" and I received the response, **"*You Know Who You Are, Angela, Angel.*"** Because I hadn't previously had much success with meditation in terms of either quieting my mind or hearing internal guidance, and because the voice seemed so otherworldly, I took notice. Several things made me certain that this wasn't my own voice talking back to me. For one, it didn't answer my question directly but told me that I already knew who I was. Second, my name isn't Angela; I had nearly forgotten that when I was about fourteen and was confirmed in the Catholic Church, I had chosen the name "Angela" as my confirmation name. I used it only for that day and then promptly forgot about it. And then, although I probably should have, I had never noticed when I chose that name at age fourteen that the name Angela contains the word "Angel."

I was mystified and curious but didn't know quite what to make of the response from my Higher Self? God? It got my attention by using language I wouldn't use normally but didn't provide a direct answer, not yet, anyway. "Coincidentally," a few days later, I was drawn to a book at my local bookstore called *Conversations with God*, by Neale Donald Walsch. Walsch, in his now internationally best-selling book, found himself receiving a stream of communication from his Higher Self or God in response to an angry letter he had dashed off to God in frustration over the way his life was not working.

As I began reading the first chapters, the words nearly jumped off the page at me. A central theme of the message received by Walsch from his Higher Self or God was that **"You Know Who You Are,"** the exact words I had heard days earlier while meditating! That got my attention. The gist of the message imparted to Walsch was that we are all essentially spiritual beings, portions of the Infinite Intelligence of the Universe or God, having an intentional physical experience for the purpose of experiencing the fullness of Being. Infinite Intelligence really couldn't experience Itself fully when all that existed was it's own pure positive energy, so this Infinite Intelligence sent out sparks or parts of Itself for the purpose of experiencing it all, the positive as well as the negative. The positive experiences couldn't fully be appreciated without something with which to contrast them. So we are those sparks of Infinite Intelligence, which were sent out into the Universe for the purpose of experiencing it all. And the central message from this Infinite Intelligence I'll call Source Energy is that we were given total freedom to create our own life experiences; we are creating our own realities by the thoughts we think and the accompanying feelings they generate. It's all up to us.

> *Our thoughts literally are real things with a magnetic energy of their own, which go out and attract things of the same vibrational frequency.*

This is the same message that has captured the attention of so many in the movie and book, "The Secret." It was astounding to me at the time and yet suddenly everything made so much sense. I could begin to see how I'd created the circumstances of my life, pleasant and unpleasant. It also confirmed to me that I could hear concrete, valid Divine Guidance and gave me greater confidence in following my own internal directives.

I would learn fairly quickly that having an intellectual understanding of how we create our own realities was not enough to dramatically change my life. Years later I was still creating fairly mixed experiences, creating mostly by default rather than very deliberately. It seemed impossible to ever get a handle on controlling or directing my thoughts. Consistency was a real problem.

Magically, about five years ago, I was introduced by a friend to the material created by Esther and Jerry Hicks and the spiritual teacher known as Abraham, which provided the missing piece of the puzzle. I highly recommend their book *Ask and It is Given*, for a complete discussion of the Law of Attraction and deliberate creation. Their teachings explained something called the "Art of Allowing," the principle of aligning your energy to allow the Law of Attraction to work on your behalf rather than against you, that is, to attract wanted rather than unwanted things into your experience.

While the teachings of Abraham changed the trajectory of my life and continue to provide cutting edge guidance, I still found, like many other Law of Attraction students, that "Allowing" my Well-Being was often easier said than done. I was still experiencing less than the joy-filled life that I knew to be possible and I was determined to find a process or program that would work to help me to maintain the higher state of vibration that I had learned was natural for me.

I decided to apply some of the analytical training I had learned at Harvard Law School and in my practice of corporate law to create and test processes and to refine processes I had learned. I wanted to develop a program that would work for myself and others, a more practical approach to creating the miracles that I knew were possible.

I read and absorbed everything I could find on deliberate creation and the Law of Attraction. I learned about creative visualization, affirmations, meditation, scripting, goal setting and myriad tools and approaches to achieving our desires. Through trial and error, I learned which processes really worked for me and began to understand why other tools so often failed. As I practiced and refined different tools for the purpose of raising my vibration, I began to achieve much more consistent results. My life began to change dramatically. Circumstances that had remained static for years shook loose and virtually every aspect of my life began to improve in ways I could hardly have imagined before. I had finally been able to break through the old patterns that had prevented me from Allowing in the Well-Being that had always been available to me.

I couldn't resist helping friends and family when I realized how well these processes worked. I was encouraged when others began to receive great results from using the tools I had refined for myself. I received strong internal directives to use my analytical, practical background to teach others what I had learned in a way that was easy to understand and apply. This course, a practical approach to working with these universal principles, is the result of following those internal directives.

I doubt that I can convey to you my full appreciation for this knowledge in my own life and my excitement in helping you to create the life you were born to live.

Law of Attraction and Allowing -The Basic Principles

You may already be very familiar with the Law of Attraction or the principle that energy attracts like energy, but I would like to be certain that we are all operating from the same understanding as a basis for using these transformational tools. Although it has not really been a secret, the movie known as *"The Secret"* brought the Law of Attraction into the mainstream and introduced many people for the first time to the concept that we are creating our own experiences with the thoughts we think.

> *We are like magnets, sending our energy out into the Universe to attract similarly vibrating energy. Positive thoughts and their accompanying vibration attract the things we want, just as negative, worrisome thoughts attract the things we're worried about.*

Realizing, for the first time, that we have more power over our experiences than we thought can be exhilarating! It is reassuring to finally understand that we are not victims of a random Universe or an arbitrary

God but are here, on purpose, with the desire to fully experience life as an extension of God or Infinite Intelligence.

Understanding that our thoughts are "things" with a magnetic power to attract into our lives both wanted and unwanted experiences can be either empowering or frustrating, however, depending upon our circumstances. When things aren't as we'd like them to be, it can be demoralizing to realize that we've created it all, leading us to wonder if we really have the ability to take control of our thoughts. Once we realize our ability to guide our thoughts, however, our incredible power as creators, we can begin to enjoy the process of creating exactly what we want! There really is nothing better than recognizing that you'd like to improve a situation and then focusing your energy on that desire and watching it come into your experience.

It was enormously helpful to me to have the process of creating our experiences broken down into discrete parts so that I clearly understood where my power lay, **what I could actually *do* to affect my own experiences**. The message of the spiritual teacher Abraham, brought forth by Jerry and Esther Hicks, helped me to understand more clearly our part in the creative process.

> *It is really a simple, three-step process to create our experiences deliberately, rather than by default. And we only really need to focus on one of them!*

As we go about our lives, without trying, we are sending out through our thoughts and feelings, a vibrational signal to the Universe of how we'd prefer that things be in our lives. Generally, we experience something or have a problem, decide that we'd like that experience to be better in some respect, and our preference is automatically communicated to the Universe through the vibration we are emitting. That part of the process was just **Step One** and required virtually no effort on our part, other than living our lives and having preferences.

In **Step Two**, Source Energy or Infinite Intelligence responds to every one of those desires or preferences. That's where the Law of Attraction comes in. Our wish for improvement or the solution to our problem is created, so to speak, energetically, and held for us in a sort of escrow known as our vibrational reality or our vortex, until we Allow it into our experience. Our desire or solution to our problem can't be pulled into our life until our vibration matches it or, at least, is in the vicinity of it, when we can begin to see evidence of its existence. Source Energy, the energy that created and maintains our world, is working with us at all times and is already responding to every desire, amassing everything needed for its fulfillment. For every problem that we've created in our lives, Source Energy has been responding simultaneously with an equal and important solution. That was the plan when we came into this world in order to have this physical experience. By participating in this physical experience we are permitting our Higher Selves, the part of us that is this same Source Energy, to experience the freedom of creating on this physical plane.

What was a breakthrough for me, despite my prior knowledge that we are creating our experiences with our thoughts, is that *all we have to do,* **our Step 3,** is to get ourselves in vibrational range with our desires by directing our thoughts more deliberately. We need to choose thoughts that cause us to feel the way we think we'll feel when we've actually achieved our desire. Then, we're a vibrational match to our desire and it's available to us. It's not as hard as it would seem, you feel better in the process, and, there are amazing tools available to help us guide our thoughts more deliberately.

In order to create the lives we were meant to live, lives of infinite possibilities, our whole job, our only job, is to raise our vibration to match the vibration of our desires. We need only make an effort to Allow the Well-Being that is natural to us. We just need to learn How to Allow.

Understanding the Concept of Allowing

When I was first exposed to the concept of Allowing, I found myself reflexively thinking that Allowing meant I just had to become comfortable with what was already in my life, good or bad, as a way of achieving happiness. The word Allowing had the association, for me, of putting up with things and finding a way to feel good about it. I've since learned that many people initially become confused by the concept of Allowing, associating the term with tolerating less than desirable circumstances and finding a way to keep a smile on your face. While making peace with where you are right now is an important part of beginning to Allow your Well-Being, Allowing in no sense means to resign yourself to putting up with the current circumstances of your life if you're not happy with them. Allowing has absolutely nothing to do with tolerating bad treatment or undesirable circumstances.

The word "Allowing," in this context, is only meant to reflect the notion that Well-Being is the predominant feature of our Universe and is natural to us. There is no stream of "Bad," only a powerful current of positive energy or Well-Being, which we can choose to line up with or not.

Allowing, therefore, is only letting happen what would happen naturally if we weren't doing something to block or disallow our alignment with Universal Energy. Allowing means to raise your vibration to a level that is in harmony with your desires and your connection to the dominant energy of Well-Being. It's that simple.

Being Aware of Your Vibration—Your Emotional Guidance System

Fortunately, we have a wonderful thing going for us in this life experience, which gives us the ability, at any moment, to be aware of how we're vibrating.

> *Our emotions are communication from our Inner Being, the part of us that is Source Energy, letting us know whether we're currently in vibrational alignment with our desires.*

Any negative emotion is a message from our Inner Being that we're creating negatively in that moment. The way we're thinking at that moment is simply not lined up with the way our Inner Being sees the situation. If our current thoughts were aligned with our intent, our fondest desires, we'd be experiencing positive emotion. So our job, whenever we feel negative emotion, is to respond to that welcome emotional indicator to move into a better way of thinking about the subject.

This understanding of how our guidance system works, however, can lead many people to become afraid of their thoughts, or feeling frustrated that they can't control them. There's really no need, however, to feel pressure to try to control our thoughts, which would be an impossible task. What we really *can* do effectively, and what is our job if we want to create the things we want in our lives, is to pay attention to how we're feeling in this moment. If we feel good, we're on track, aligned with our intentions. If we feel negative emotion, no big deal, thoughts don't manifest into things immediately. There is time to choose a thought that feels better. By working with our emotional guidance system we don't need to worry about controlling our thoughts; we need only guide our thoughts to ones that feel better.

There is a buffer of time in our world where it takes quite a bit of negative thinking to create an undesired outcome. Positive energy or positive thinking, on the other hand, creates more quickly because it is so many times more powerful than negative energy. It is said that one person who is in alignment with Source Energy is more powerful than millions of people who are not.

> *We can be much more relaxed when we experience our inevitable negative emotion when we understand how exponentially more powerful our positive vibration can be, and that we have the power, at every moment, to shift into better feeling thoughts and a higher vibration. **All of our power lies in the present moment.***

Shifting into a higher vibration from where you are should always feel like *relief.* When you consider the wide range of emotions a person could experience, you can appreciate how you might change your thinking to move up the emotional scale and, in the process, raise your vibration. At the bottom range of human emotions you'd find the feelings of despair or fear or depression, which have the characteristic of a sense of powerlessness. When someone finds himself in a state of despair, the path to relief would likely be to a feeling of anger. While anger is not an emotion that we'd like to hold onto for any extended period, it is a step up from despair inasmuch as it provides a feeling of regaining your power.

The notion here is that it would be difficult, if not impossible, to jump from despair into happiness or joy. It's just an impossible leap to make immediately. The goal, in this case, would be to move as quickly as possible through the feeling of anger into another feeling which would again provide some relief, perhaps frustration. Once you moved into feeling merely frustrated about the situation, you might talk yourself into feeling just overwhelmed and from there it is a fairly short trip to feeling optimistic or hopeful and a much more positive vibration. From there you'd be attracting a whole different quality of circumstances.

To give a short example of how someone might gradually move themselves up the emotional scale, providing a sense of relief and a higher vibration, let's consider the case of someone who is feeling a sense of despair or fear about losing their job due to a recent round of lay-offs. The feeling of despair would involve fearful thoughts about losing their job, not finding another job, being destitute. That negative emotion would be a clear signal that Source Energy did not view the situation that way, that there is a better, more optimistic way of seeing the situation that would yield much better results. Source Energy, instead is aligned with the solution to the problem, which has already been created in the person's vibrational reality.

In an effort to guide their thinking to better feeling thoughts, the employee might think about what a good job they've done for the company, how qualified they are and how deserving of the job. That could lead them directly to a feeling of anger or blame, a step up from despair. In a state of anger, they'd begin to focus on their own worthiness and how they wouldn't be in that situation if someone else hadn't messed up! While they wouldn't want to languish in anger, it would certainly feel better than feeling fearful and powerless and they'd already be emitting a higher vibration.

After bucking themselves up by reminding themselves of how deserving they are of their job, they might begin to feel more confident and begin to see more clearly that there were many people who brought about the economic conditions that put their company in a weakened state. They might feel less angry with their boss, their fellow employees, and merely feel overwhelmed by the situation. Again, frustration and overwhelm are higher states of vibration than anger and blame and will attract better results.

Now, this person might begin to focus on some of their better experiences at their job, the good job they'd done on particular projects, the times they were appreciated for their efforts. This person is gradually moving himself up the emotional scale to a higher vibration. The goal would be to continue guiding their thoughts to a point where they might either feel more secure about their job or feel confident about finding another job, a vibration of hope, another step up the emotional scale. Once this individual guides their thoughts to this better feeling vibration, and is able to maintain that as their dominant vibration on that subject, they are now positioned to attract a much better outcome to their job situation than when they were mired in feelings of despair. Now they're creating deliberately.

> *Your emotions, positive or negative, are valuable feedback from the Universe that can help you develop a greater awareness of your relationship with your Inner Being. They are always there for you, always guiding you, and your thoughts can always be changed to provide a feeling of relief, which puts you on track to a higher vibration.*

Now that we've covered these basics of deliberate creation, the remainder of this course is devoted to those tools which can help you to be more aware of your emotional guidance, to reach for better feeling thoughts more easily, and to raise your vibration more consistently to a level where you're able to manifest the things you want, to consciously create your life experience.

So, let's get started!!

Introduction to the System—The Daily Tools

While I would love to launch immediately into using the two Daily Tools which I believe will begin to create positive results in your life very quickly, it is important to have a foundation for understanding why the Daily Tools are so effective in raising and maintaining your vibration. Shifting your vibration is based on very subtle differences in your attitude and thoughts and it is important to appreciate these subtle differences in order for the Tools to work their magic.

The two Daily Tools, Tuning Up Your Vibration and Going Within, will be introduced in Lessons 4 and 5. They form the foundation for the course.

In the next three lessons, however, we are laying a foundation for the foundation, so please be patient because they are the key, in my experience, to allowing the Basic Tools to work properly.

So, let's enjoy laying the foundation!

Lesson One: Making One Decision

Armed with the knowledge that you're creating everything in your life as a result of the way you're vibrating, it's easy to be motivated to change your way of thinking. Of course, that can be easier said than done. Without any strategies for guiding our thoughts, many people, despite knowing about the Law of Attraction, find it difficult to make any lasting changes in their lives. Our patterns of thought, our beliefs, have developed over our lifetimes and can require some effort to change. Most of us have a mixed vibration on most subjects, managing to be optimistic or hopeful at times, and falling into frustration or even despair on the same subject, depending upon the circumstances. Most of us are in the habit of reacting to our circumstances, rather than making a conscious choice to feel the way we want to feel regardless of the situation.

The job of managing your vibration needs to be viewed as your whole job, your most important job, if you really are to create any positive changes in your life experience. While making an effort to think more positively will generate some positive momentum in terms of the things you're attracting into your life, real creative control requires a fundamental commitment to choosing the best thoughts available to you or making feeling good your highest priority. Your one decision needs to be that feeling as good as you can, maintaining the purest vibration you can on the subjects that matter, is the guiding principle of your life.

> *You need to make a commitment that you are not just willing to **try to** choose the best thoughts that you're able to conjure at any moment, but that you **will** choose the best thoughts that are available to you whenever you become aware of negative emotion.*

In my own case, the decision to make feeling good my highest priority, choosing the best thoughts I can find, has been the single most important decision I've made. Everything began to shift for the better once I decided that feeling good was my guiding principle. It took a dramatic situation for me to finally realize that I had no choice but to make feeling as good as possible my highest priority. I had recently moved cross-country with my family and was feeling bereft having left my extended family and many close friends on the opposite coast. In my feelings of loneliness and isolation I realized that nothing would change as long as I continued to haphazardly just "try to" think more positively. It was then that I decided that choosing the best thoughts I could about my situation had to be my top priority if I was to re-create my life in new surroundings.

I was in a completely new place where I knew no one, but I realized that if I wanted new friendships, I needed to raise my vibration by appreciating the relationships I had in my life already. I could appreciate the friends and family who were at a distance. I could appreciate the relationships I had with my husband and each of my kids. I realized I didn't have the luxury of focusing on any lack in my life, a negative vibration, if I really wanted to create the life I wanted in my new surroundings.

Amazingly, unless you know the way the laws work, upon making my decision to guide my thoughts to an appreciation of the relationships I already had in my life, I was almost immediately introduced to a new friend by an acquaintance, someone with whom I had an instant connection. Then that same afternoon a fellow mother with whom I'd only shared carpooling duties, stopped to chat and confided a story she needed to share which was actually really helpful for me to hear. When she walked away, she said, "I'm so glad we got to talk, I love you!" She subsequently became one of my closest friends on the west coast. This all happened within a day.

My decision to choose the best thoughts I could by committing to a positive focus on the relationships I already had in my life resulted in an almost immediate attraction of new friends. Although this occurred before I began using the Daily Tools described in this course, it was the beginning of my understanding of the incredible power of my focus. Making my one decision to feel good as often as possible and focusing on my desire to make new connections, resulted in a nearly instantaneous shift in my point of attraction.

When you think about it, the only reason we have any goals or desires at all is that we think that, in the attainment of them, it will make us feel better. There isn't a desire out there to the contrary. It simplifies things when we focus on feeling better, choosing to think of our situation in the best way we can at the moment, regardless of the circumstances. This one decision both simplifies the process of learning to Allow and helps you to stay on track while you still haven't seen evidence of your goal. This one decision helps you to avoid getting so caught up in the dramas of life, particularly the dramas of others, because you realize that doing so would undermine your ability to feel as good as you can whenever you can.

> *The notion that feeling good should be your highest priority may sound selfish until you recognize that it's the very best thing you could ever do, not only for yourself, but also for the people you care about.*

You've undoubtedly heard the wisdom that unless you take care of yourself first, you have nothing to give others. When you think of that concept in terms of vibration, it becomes clearer as to why that concept holds true. As we'll discuss later in this course in connection with relationships, when you raise your vibration, you become like a radio tower for your family, friends, and everyone in your orbit. Your higher vibration causes you to bring out the best in the people you're focused upon. You literally uplift them by choosing to make generating good feelings *your* highest priority!

I cannot stress strongly enough how this one decision, to make feeling good, choosing the best way of thinking you have access to on all of the subjects in your life, needs to be your highest priority. As a practical matter, this involves constantly checking in with yourself to see how you're feeling. You'll remember that your emotions are your guidance from your Higher Self, telling you how you're vibrating. Good feelings equal a positive vibration. Negative feelings mean you need to stop, appreciate your new awareness, and choose a thought that feels better. How you're feeling is your Higher Self telling you whether your perception of a situation is lined up with the way your Source sees it. If it feels joyful, exciting, hopeful, in the realm of positive emotions, you're connected with the energy that is helping you to get everything you want, from a parking space to a loving relationship, to financial freedom.

Anything less, anything that doesn't feel good,

from frustration to anger, to fear or worry, means only that you need to re-direct your thoughts to the best thought you can come up with at the moment. The good news is that your new thoughts don't have to be extremely positive thoughts, just ones that provide some relief, some improvement in the way you feel. In fact, when you're feeling in the lower range of emotions it's nearly impossible to jump into extremely positive thinking because your thoughts are attracting similarly vibrating negative thoughts. So, all you can do is choose a thought which feels a bit better. And, if you can hold onto that better way of thinking for even seventeen seconds, you'll have created a different point of attraction which will attract to you better and better feeling thoughts.

A helpful way of viewing this process and of shifting to better thoughts is first to remember that **all of your power is right now**. Your point of power is always in the present. It's where all of your energy lies. No matter where you are, what may have brought you to this point, you have the power right now to shift your vibration and begin attracting better circumstances. As soon as you become aware that you're feeling negative emotion, rather than beating yourself up for negative thinking, congratulate yourself for being more tuned into your emotional guidance. Now that you know that a solution has been created at the same time as your problem, use that awareness as positive momentum to propel you into alignment with your vibrational reality where your solution is waiting for you.

When you become aware that you're feeling bored or angry or frustrated, stop and think of what thoughts just generated that feeling. Then think of how you'd like to feel instead of bored or angry or frustrated and focus on those good feelings.

For example, in the case of feeling frustration over something that hasn't gone your way, realize that this clearly isn't the way Source views this situation or you wouldn't be feeling frustrated. Remind yourself that you enjoy feeling atpeace, feeling contented, feeling appreciative of the good things in your life. Think about what makes you feel at peace and what you appreciate in your life and milk those feelings for a while. Realize that improvement in this situation is already available in your vibrational reality right now if you can re-focus your thinking. Talk yourself down. Find the positives in the situation, remind yourself that the situation is temporary, nothing is more important than your vibration, especially this thing over which you're frustrated. Feel your way forward into those better feelings that are a match to your desires and your solution.

A decision to make every effort to do just this will begin to change the circumstances of your life as soon as that day, because you've shifted your point of attraction. Things must begin to improve. It's a law of the Universe and it's consistent.

What may be becoming apparent as we talk about raising our vibration to the level of our desires by choosing better feeling thoughts, is that the key to deliberate creation is **feeling the way you think you'll feel when you've manifested your desire, before your desire has manifested**. Many of us are creatures of habit when it comes to our thinking, and carry around limiting beliefs about what is really possible in our lives; this can make it difficult to make the leap of faith that would allow us to maintain a consistently positive, confident focus, expecting good things, before there is any concrete evidence of good things showing up.

This inability to focus on the good that's already been created for us, without real evidence of its existence, is what presents the stumbling block to creating on purpose for most of us. You could call it the Catch-22 of creating your own reality. You need to create the positive expectation, feel as if you already have what you want, before you can have it. And, when you feel as if you already have it, you must get it. That's the way the laws work. Yet, for most people, it seems impossible to feel happy and full of positive expectation before they've received what it is they really want. It can seem difficult to have faith in a positive outcome when you're surrounded predominantly by what you don't want.

But, you should know, because I've seen the evidence in my life and in the lives of others who've made the decision to make feeling good their highest priority, it's absolutely possible to make this kind of shift in your vibration before you've fixed what's broken in your life. There are tools that can help you to begin creating more of the things you've been hoping for, which will give you the **BELIEF**, and eventually the **KNOWING**, that you can have whatever you want. You've already created it for yourself by being willing to be part of this physical experience and express your desires; you just need to raise your vibration to match it. It's yours!

It's about time to start playing the game with more than just a vague understanding of the laws of the Universe. The laws hold your solutions and your results. You need only make one decision, that is, that the most important thing in your life is to feel good by choosing the best thoughts you can. From there, anything is possible!

Lesson One Practice

Make your one decision to change your life. Don't just say you're going to *try to* make feeling good your highest priority, but that you *are going to* make feeling good your highest priority. Do you recognize the important difference between the statements "I'm going to try to lose that ten pounds," and "I'm going to lose that ten pounds"?

Because I've learned that there is tremendous power in putting your thoughts in writing, which we'll go into in more detail when we get to the Daily Tools, I'm going to ask that you commit to your one decision in writing. The act of writing sharpens your focus and makes your commitment more real, more substantial, easier to remember and maintain.

I strongly urge you in this Practice to make a contract with yourself along the lines of the contract that follows. Definitely feel free to edit the language to something that sounds more like your own voice or resonates more strongly with you. But, whatever you do, commit to your one decision, that choosing thoughts that make you feel as good as possible is your highest priority. By making your one decision you're signaling to the Universe your true intention. And, the Universe won't let you down. It's nothing but supportive of your intentions.

When you commit to feeling good, the Universe will match you up with the things, people and ideas that are a vibrational match to your commitment. Once you've made this one decision, you've already begun to attract evidence of your Well-Being and the vast support of the Universe will begin showing itself to you.

CONTRACT

I,_____, commit to making feeling good and choosing the best thoughts that are available to me my highest priority. I realize that by choosing to feel good, as often as possible, I am harnessing the energy of the Universe for my benefit and that of all of those with whom I interact. I choose to feel as good as I can, knowing it is my life purpose as a creator in this physical experience. And, my commitment to expansion benefits us all.

_____
(Signature)

Lesson Two: Setting Your Intentions

We discussed the three-step process of creating deliberately and concluded that your real work is Step 3 of the process, or lining up your energy to match the higher vibration of your desires. Step One, or sending your desire out to the Universe, happens more or less automatically every time you develop a preference that you'd like something to be better.

You're at work, for example, and find yourself thinking that you'd like to have more independence in your position or be compensated more generously for what you do. Boom, as soon as you think that thought, it's sent out to be responded to by the vast intelligence of the Universe. Your preference for something better, whatever it may be, is sent forth as soon as you can dream it up. As soon as your preference is emitted, the Universe takes care of Step 2 as it begins to orchestrate all of the people, events and circumstances that will fulfill your desire. Step 2 is not something to be taken lightly.

> *Can you really appreciate the fact that the Universe is at work on your behalf, all of the time, to match you up with literally anything that you desire?*

Once you fully appreciate the generosity of the cooperative Universe, it becomes easier to relax and do your real work, which is Step 3. Again, your only work is to raise your vibration to match your desire so that it can be pulled into your experience.

Sometimes it is amazing to me, even now, how beautifully our desires are communicated to the Universe, when we don't realize we're focusing on them. I've learned that they really only need to be sent out once in order for the Universe to respond to them. In fact, it is just that sort of easy focus on our desire, coupled with an effort to keep returning to good feeling thoughts, which seems to create most effectively.

In a funny example, the Universe delivered something to me before I even remembered that I had been looking for it. Over the years, I've always purchased inexpensive Advent calendars for my kids. When they were younger they loved the cardboard calendars where each day in the month of December you would open a cardboard flap to reveal a piece of chocolate candy. When our family spent a few years on the west coast, however, I found it difficult to find the calendars. The stores where I had purchased them didn't exist on the west coast and similar stores didn't always stock the calendars.

Eventually, during those few years, I would sometimes find them somewhere as it got very close to Christmas, usually defeating the idea of opening the windows each day for the month of December. This year, however, I hadn't thought about the calendars, as I hadn't yet really focused on the holidays. As I was shopping just prior to Thanksgiving, pushing my cart through the aisle of a local grocery store, I inadvertently bumped the corner of some kind of display with my cart. Things started falling down in front of me and, as I bent down to pick them up, I realized they were the Advent calendars!

I laughed as I chose three of them for my kids, not quite believing what had happened, and placed them in the small section at the front of my cart. The funniest part, though, was that after I finished cleaning up the other calendars, which had fallen on the floor, I glanced into my cart and realized that exactly three calendars had already fallen into the larger basket of my cart! I just love it when the Universe surprises me in ways I hadn't imagined and gives me evidence of my ability to line up my energy.

While your desires are constantly being communicated to the Universe without a concerted effort on your part, I have seen that it can be helpful to have a clear idea of where you'd like to see yourself in the various areas of your life. These are the goals that get us out of bed in the morning and give us a sense of purpose. Choosing some important desires that we'd like to manifest can also give us a sense of focus and direction while we're looking for ways to make ourselves feel good as often as possible. While you don't need a detailed list of goals in order to make the Universe aware of your desires, having a sense of direction does help you to stay more motivated in lining up your vibration with your desires.

Having a basic sense of where we'd like to see ourselves, general goals, gives us that feeling of purposefulness that calls forth more of the life-giving positive energy of our Source.

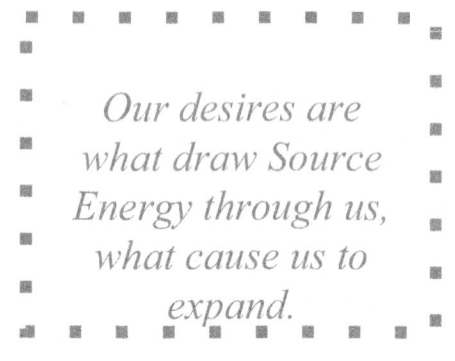

> *Our desires are what draw Source Energy through us, what cause us to expand.*

So, while the Universe may have a clear idea of our preferences and is constantly working to fulfill them, it's a good idea to come up with our own list of things we'd like to create.

Often the best way of honing in on our desires is to make a list of the things that aren't working in our lives, the things we'd like to change. Perhaps because most of us have been taught to focus on our problems and to solve them before we can be happy, it's been proven that it's easier for most people to create their list of desires by beginning with a list of problems in their lives.

Don't worry, very little time will actually be spent dwelling on this list so as not to activate the vibration of what we ***don't want***. So, in this part of the course we're going to make a list, to be used only briefly, of the things that aren't working in our lives. After creating that list, for each item we'll make a list of its opposite. You'll find that this process helps you to easily come up with a list of your most important desires.

Typical examples of things that aren't working for many people which could form the list of "don't wants," are living paycheck to paycheck, relationship problems, unfulfilling work, lack of purpose, a body which doesn't feel great, a home which falls short of their ideal. You get the idea. Now, the opposite of these things which could stand improvement would be financial security or freedom, a happy, supportive relationship, a job you love, clarity about your life purpose, a fit, healthy body, a nurturing beautiful home.

So, as the practical application of your new approach at the end of this Lesson, you'll be asked to come up with this same list of a few things that aren't working in your life and then, on the other side of the page, to create a list of their opposite. Although there is no limit to the number of things you could put on your list, one important part of this program is that you not feel overwhelmed with goals or processes. That can lead to the feeling that you're not doing enough, and that Allowing is hard work. You understand now that viewing the processes as complicated or feeling that you're not doing enough would only create a negative vibration that is out of sync with the pure positive vibration of your desires. Our goal here, and throughout this course, is to keep it simple!

I'd like to suggest listing just a few "don't wants," which will be used to create your list of goals. At this juncture, choose desires that seem fairly attainable, ones that you feel fairly comfortable that you can accomplish. That way, you're unlikely to feel overwhelmed and more likely to see quick results, which will give you your own evidence of your ability to attract your desires.

I'd also like to add one caveat to my suggestion that you create a short list of goals that seem fairly attainable to you. Later in the course, when we move into using our first Daily Tool, we'll have a more detailed discussion about the option of making your desires general or very specific. You may have heard, for example, of someone pasting a photo of a red sports car on his or her wall and using their focus to attract the exact red sports car they had pictured. That kind of focus works beautifully for many people but can have the opposite effect on others.

The only rule here about how specific to be with your desires, is that they be only as specific as will generate a good feeling when you think about them. If listing a certain beautiful car gives you a feeling of excitement and belief that it is possible, go for it. If, on the other hand, when you think of the new car, you begin to think of all of the reasons why you probably won't get it, you're being too specific. At least at this juncture, you're not easily able to create a vibration that matches the new car. It would be better, in that case, to list a more general desire of having more financial abundance in your life, in an amount that creates excitement but doesn't create doubts about your ability to attract it into your life.

Have fun with creating your list and include things that bring a smile to your face when you think about them. Don't worry about including everything you desire now because we are beginning to create momentum at this point in the process.

> *When you've experienced how the laws work and seen evidence of your ability to create what you want, you'll develop the belief and, eventually, the knowing, that there really are no limits to what you can create.*

If you can use your power of focus to create even one thing you desire in your life, you'll develop the confidence that these same principles will allow you to reach your bigger goals, which may have seemed more out of range before you understood the process. You'll begin to see that anything is possible!

Lesson Two Practice

On the left side of the page, make a list of the "don't wants" in your life, which you'll focus on only briefly. Then, after you've completed the list, use them to create your list of goals on the other side of the page. You'll see how easy it is to come up with a list of desires from that brief focus on the things you'd like to change in your life.

Now, narrow your list down to a few important general desires, preferably ones in which you have more confidence of your ability to draw them into your life. Remember, this is an ongoing process, which is never done, so you'll always have the opportunity to add more goals after you've manifested some of the desires on your initial list. Some fairly quick evidence of attracting something you want will help you to be even more confident in the process and your own ability as a deliberate creator. Some wants could be: being able to pay my bills more easily, having more fun in my relationship, having a well-maintained home, having a more fit, healthy body.

While I've stressed choosing a few goals that seem within reach right now, I want to be clear that, in the long run, you'll find that there are no limits to what you can create and that you should reach for literally anything you want. I'd just like for you to build some confidence in the process and your own ability to get your momentum going. As you're focusing on what it is you'd like to create, it's important to feel that not only would it be fun to achieve those desires, but that, whatever they are, they're your birthright, you deserve them!

The way I like to think of our desires is that no desire is undeserving of manifestation; every desire we have is the desire of our Source for more complete expression. We wouldn't have the desire if it wouldn't lead to our expansion or if we didn't have the talent or ability to attain it. Our desires are the basis of our growth, what pulls the current of Source through us. There should never be any doubt that you deserve to have everything you desire. You wouldn't want to deny the experience to Source Energy would you? Great, now take some time to come up with a list that creates some excitement for you.

Things I Don't Want:

_____
_____
_____
_____
_____
_____
_____
_____
_____

Things I'll Create Instead:

_____
_____
_____
_____
_____
_____
_____
_____
_____
_____

I'd like to take this process a step further now that you've come up with a preliminary list of your goals or intentions. In order to move into an even better feeling vibration when it comes to your goals, I'd like to ask you to think about **_why_** you want each of the things you want, **_how you think achieving each desire will make you feel._**

When you focus purely on your desire, your vibration may be mixed. You're likely still focusing, at least partially, on the fact that you don't yet have it. Reflecting on the "why," that is, how you think achieving your desire will make you feel, on the other hand, moves you into that pure positive energy which is a match to the vibration of your desire.

So, for each of your goals, write down exactly how you think achieving that goal will make you feel. For example, attracting a new relationship into your life might make you feel more secure, confident, more loving. As you go though the process of writing down why you want each of your goals, you should feel a sense of relief, a shift into more positive emotion. You might even feel a tingle as you think about why you want to create those things in your life. Take your time and enjoy the process and then we'll move into the next Lesson.

My Intentions or Desires:

(Beneath each intention write down why you want to achieve that desire, how you think having it in your life will make you feel.)

Lesson Three: Laying Your Foundation—Making Peace with Where You Are

> There is nothing more conducive to the building or maintaining of momentum than making peace with where you are.
>
> Abraham

I know that I've insisted that the two Daily Tools are both the cornerstones of this course and the key ingredients to learning to Allow your Well-Being more consistently. While I've seen that these two practices are indeed the way to raise and maintain a more pure vibration, a very necessary foundation must be laid for using these daily practices. Your jumping off point needs to be established and that starting point involves feeling okay with where you find yourself at this moment in time. I've personally seen for myself and in the lives of others that simply making peace with where you are right now, without taking any other action, often results in a dramatic shift in the direction of your life.

In one of the most amazing and clearest examples I've seen, a client I'll call Renee, after years of wondering why she couldn't attract a lasting relationship into her life, attracted her perfect mate within weeks of making peace with her life as it was. Renee had married shortly after graduating from college and her marriage had ended in divorce after a few years. Over a number of years after her divorce, Renee had several relationships, none of which resulted in the long-term soul mate relationship she was looking for. As years went by, it began to appear to Renee that marriage might never happen, despite her sending out her request to the Universe as clearly and as often as she could. She was familiar with the Law of Attraction and, knowing what she knew, she couldn't understand why it wasn't happening for her. Her vibration was basically permanently in the state of Step 1 of the process (asking), never really moving into the higher vibration that would match her desire for her perfect mate.

In what was a subtle shift in her thinking, however, she found herself observing her friends, many of whom were in less than happy marriages, and thinking, "Well, I actually have a good life even in comparison to my married friends. I have a great, high paying job, travel, friends and family who care about me. I'd still like to meet that guy and have kids but, I do have a good life right now." She didn't let go of her desire but she softened it from the tone of "Why, why, why isn't it happening for me?" to "I'd still like that but I'm happy with where I am." Within a few weeks, Renee found herself dating a colleague from her company whom she had only noticed casually before. He simply wasn't visible to her as long as she was maintaining her lower vibration of frustration. Once she made peace with where she was, what was previously out of range became visible to her, and he turned out to be her loving, devoted husband.

The power of making peace with where you are cannot be overstated. Before we can begin to raise our vibration to match our desires, we need to feel okay with the temporary place where we've arrived at this moment. Otherwise, even if we try to focus on our new desires, our vibration is continually muddied with thoughts of "Why am I here? How did I let this happen? I can't be happy as long as I'm in this situation." With those underlying thoughts, you'd be constantly emitting a vibration of frustration or regret rather than the hopefulness or optimism that is a closer match to your desires.

As I mentioned in our discussion of the definition of Allowing, I'd like to remind you that the word toleration does not come into play here. In making peace with where you are, you are not tolerating less than you deserve or condoning bad treatment from people who cause trouble in your life. The concept of making peace, rather involves a realization that you are responsible for your own creations and that you can get to wherever you want to be from wherever you are right now.

Making peace with where you are also involves an appreciation for the fact that the Universe is always working on your desires. Once you understand how the laws work, that you indeed have the power to use your energy to be, do or have anything you desire, you can relax into the knowing that where you are now is okay. There is no better place to begin than where you are because it's caused you to launch the very desires that are drawing Source Energy through you at this very moment. Without the experiences that have caused you to emit so many desires, the wonderful creations that are merely awaiting your cooperation would not be possible.

In attempting to come to the place where you are at peace with where you are, one important realization might come into play. I've seen this realization serve as a tipping point that has helped a number of people to make peace with where they are when they found themselves in difficult circumstances. When someone has gone through a particularly stressful situation and finds him or herself far from where they'd like to be, it could take a bit more effort to reach that feeling of "everything is okay with where I am." You want to make peace and move on, but might still be beating yourself up for allowing yourself to arrive at this place, which is far from where you want to be. You're more focused on the fact that mistakes have been made, by you, and if you hadn't made those poor decisions or allowed certain things to happen you wouldn't be in this situation.

One helpful way of looking at the situation when you find it hard to let go of your judgments about where you find yourself is to realize that ***nothing has gone wrong here***. This can be just the sort of realization that really cleans up your vibration and allows you to send out that pure vibration which is a match to your desires. As long as we think mistakes have been made for which we blame ourselves or others, it's impossible to send out a pure positive vibration.

This was a powerful realization for me, which finally helped me to be at peace and clean up my vibration on some long-standing issues. I hadn't realized that beneath my surface hopefulness about my future, my underlying story was, "How did I get here" I should've known better. If I hadn't made this decision, none of these things would have happened." One day, as I realized I was still having those thoughts beneath my thoughts, I had an epiphany, which has since served me well. I questioned my underlying thoughts, which were only operating to sabotage my desire to send out a pure positive vibration.

I asked myself how I would feel if I realized that nothing has gone wrong here? I knew that I would feel completely differently about the situation, so much more at peace. I asked myself, "How do I know that any of these decisions were mistakes? How do I know what my Higher Self might have intended for me to have in my experience? How do I know that things would have worked out differently or better if I had chosen different options? Hadn't the contrasting experiences put more and better things in my vibrational escrow? Hadn't this challenge resulted in my learning How to Allow? Would I ever have had all of the wonderful things I have in my life right now if I hadn't dove into the experiences that caused me to learn so much?" I think not!

> *If you can come to the place where you trust that a loving Universe is constantly guiding you and that nothing has gone wrong here, you can make peace with where you are right now and know that everything will be okay. Without the contrary underlying thoughts, mountains can be moved. A huge shift in your vibration is an inevitable result of accepting that nothing has gone wrong here. You'll realize that where you are right now is fine and you can go anywhere from here.*

Making peace with where you are, at its core, involves invoking the high vibration of the emotion of **appreciation**. Appreciation is at the top of our emotional range and is pure, positive vibration. No matter what your circumstances, there are some things to appreciate about most of the aspects of your life. If you find yourself far from where you want to be and can find little to appreciate in your present circumstances, you might need to begin by appreciating the fact that you now understand the ways that the laws work and have the power to make changes in your life. You can appreciate the fact that you've re-claimed your power, which is no small thing!

A profound shift in my own circumstances occurred when I finally made peace with where I was and I sometimes still can hardly believe how many things lined up to allow me to manifest my desire. As I had mentioned previously, our family had made a decision to move to the west coast, in what was to be a temporary move related to my husband's work. For a variety of reasons, the move proved not to be temporary and our family spent five years on the west coast. While there were many happy moments for our family there, I dearly missed the family and friends we had left behind on the east coast.

Because of our children's school commitments, it was difficult to make a move. We reached a critical juncture when two of our children would be making transitions to different schools and it seemed that it was now or never if we were to return to the east coast. I very much wanted to return and yet my desire was conditioned on the fact that it be a good move for everyone else in the family. As the Mom, I could not imagine being happy with a move that did not fit for the rest of my family.

There were so many conditions that would have to conspire for us to be able to move, my husband's work situation, the attitude of the rest of the family toward moving, my sons' admissions to various schools, the sale of our home, finding another new home, any one of which could have de-railed any prospective relocation to the east coast. I realized that many of those factors were outside of my control and that I would really need to finally make peace with our location on the west coast. I still wanted to return to family and friends in the east, but I decided that I could be at peace with where I was on the west coast. I could appreciate the friends and positive aspects of our life on the west coast and that would lead to my landing in the best place for our family. I realized that choosing to appreciate the west coast would not necessarily force me to remain there if I didn't choose to, it would just raise my vibration to match the best location for me and my family. I realized that only by being happy with what I had, could I attract any improvement in my circumstances.

I decided that if conditions caused us to remain on the west coast for several more years, I would make the very best of it there and would find a way to stay more connected with family and friends on the east coast. I would find a way to be more bi-coastal, perhaps finding work that would allow me to stay in closer contact with my loved ones on the east coast. I would stay hopeful about moving east if it was in the best interests of all of us and would find the best aspects of where I was on the west coast. It was a subtle, yet very important, shift in the way I viewed my situation and the vibration I was emitting to the Universe.

In what seemed like a miracle at the time, my sons were both admitted to schools of their choice on the east coast, my older son chose to attend an east coast school rather than a school on the west coast, my husband jumped on board and thought it would be a good move for our family, we sold our house in a difficult market for a healthy profit, we found a new home within weeks of our moving date, and our former housekeeper on the east coast even had the week off when we moved into our new home and was able to help us get settled.

> *When you make peace with where you are, the Universe works to line up all of the details necessary to manifest your desire.*

Making peace with where you are, of course, works on a smaller scale as well. It seems almost too easy to be true, but once you're okay with where you are, you'll find that little things begin to line up for you. When you're driving to work or school and find yourself appreciating your reliable car, the sunny day, the fact that you understand how the laws of the Universe work, you'll find yourself getting that parking space, avoiding traffic snarls and arriving on time. These little things, seemingly unimportant, are the kinds of things that happen often when you begin to shift your vibration to a higher level.

I'm still amazed at times at the surprising support that results from feeling at peace with where you are and making a real effort to feel good as often as possible. The strangest things will happen to me and I almost need to pinch myself, to remind myself to appreciate every last bit of it!!

I was recently shopping for the holidays and had gone to a large department store and purchased some gifts for my daughter. I was feeling good, excited about buying gifts for my family and in the holiday spirit. The store was having a promotion where you were given a fifteen-dollar gift certificate for every one hundred dollars spent, to be used at a later date. I had purchased several items and was eligible for three of the fifteen-dollar certificates. Although I should have received only three of the fifteen-dollar coupons, the woman at the counter looked at me with a big smile on her face and said, "I'm going to give you one of these instead." I was surprised to see that it was a two hundred dollar gift certificate with no strings attached. It only needed to be used in the women's clothing department at some future date. Not a problem!

But the story gets better. A couple of weeks later, I realized that the coupon was to expire the next day and thought I'd better redeem it. Coincidentally, I had recently thought that I really needed a new wool jacket of some kind. I had pictured a brown wool or cashmere short jacket. As I went into the store, I noticed on the sale rack that there was a beautiful dark brown cashmere short jacket (only one in just my size). It was exactly what I had imagined but even better. It had also been marked down from $495 to $240. With my gift from the Universe, my two hundred dollar certificate, I happily purchased my perfect jacket for forty dollars. I still don't understand why the very kind woman at the sales counter gave me the $200 coupon, but I've learned not to question these wonderful gifts.

Finding things to appreciate in the life you have will continue to be a theme of this course and I would encourage you to take time to assess where you are, focusing on the most positive aspects of each area of your life. Finding things to appreciate in your current circumstances and in your daily round will begin to attract more of the things that match that vibration of appreciation. You'll also be re-programming your thinking to gravitate more toward thoughts of appreciation, in general, an important component of raising your vibration.

And, the most important way to begin that shift is deciding to find the best things you can think of about your circumstances right now. That you have friends, a job, a spouse who loves you, a roof over your head, good food in your refrigerator, loyal pets, are all worthy of appreciation. Almost every area in your life has some things that can be appreciated and it's time to begin to focus upon them. So, in this practical application of what we've learned, I'd like to ask you to make a list of the major areas of your life and, in each case, as many things as you can think of that are cause for appreciation.

I'm hoping that this exercise will lead you to a feeling of relief, the sense that it's okay that I'm where I am right now and that everything can get better and better.

> ***Remember that nothing has gone wrong here.*** *Armed with the knowledge of how the laws of the Universe work, you can get to anywhere you choose from here. This knowing can, and should, form an important basis for making peace with where you are right now.*

Lesson Three Practice

Think of the important areas of your life. Some suggestions include relationships, health, finances, work or creative outlet, spirituality. Feel free to add any other areas that are important to you. For each area, list as many things as you can think of that you appreciate. This exercise is laying the foundation for beginning to shift your point of attraction to a higher set point. I would not be surprised at all if you began to experience evidence of positive creations after going through this exercise. Again, making peace with where you are, appreciating what has brought you to this place where you are taking control of creating your reality, is the first step in beginning to Allow in the Well-Being that you've always intended.

Health

_____
_____
_____
_____
_____

Finances

Work or Creative Outlet

Spirituality

Relationships

Lesson Four: The First Daily Tool—Tuning Up Your Vibration

While I have found a multitude of tools that can work for some of the people some of the time, I've learned that inconsistently using a wide variety of tools usually results in still having a pretty mixed vibration. Despite using our best efforts, we use the tools we've learned only when we think of it or have the time. When we remember, we might recite affirmations, visualize, or make a vision board. We may think we've ramped up our vibration when our experiences demonstrate quite the contrary. Often, while we think we're focusing on our desire, we're mostly focusing on the fact that we don't yet have it.

The other downside of trying to use a multitude of manifestation tools in a scattershot fashion, is that it can lead to a feeling that we're not doing enough, that we haven't used certain tools which we know we should be using more often. This may create the feeling that we're not working hard enough at this and, therefore, we can't expect any real results. Or we may just conclude that we're lousy creators on the basis of our spotty results.

> *These feelings that we're not doing enough, that it all has to be hard work, or that we're just not good at it, are all contrary to the vibration that we're hoping to achieve, that is, a relaxed expectation that our desires are already on their way to us.*

There are lots of good manifestation tools out there and I definitely would not discourage anyone from using any tool that they've found to be fun and effective. Before I committed to using the two Daily Tools, however, I found myself having an inner dialogue along the following lines:

"Ugh, I really need to create that vision board; that would help me to focus more. Why haven't I done that? I should do it, I just don't feel that excited about doing it. I'm just not doing enough. My negative thoughts are definitely outweighing my positive thoughts. I'm not remembering to pre-pave the segments of my day. Gotta start doing that! I really need to write down some good affirmations and use them a few times a day. I've got to get on that! Oh no, there I go again rehashing that problem I'm having with him. No wonder the situation isn't improving. I really need to spend

fifteen minutes a day picturing that relationship just the way I want it to be. Why don't I do that? Ugh, sometimes it's just so hard to do that. I should be keeping a gratitude journal. Didn't Oprah say she does that?

I could go on but you probably get the idea. It can be almost as if having too many tools is dangerous, although that need not be the case. Being aware of lots of tools is fine, particularly if it leads you to think about the essence of the tools, and why they could or could not work for you, depending upon your beliefs and expectations. What I believe is essential to really mastering **How to Allow**, however, is committing to two basic practices that you'll do each day.

> *We tend to respond well to rituals, activities we look forward to and don't require much thought. And, these rituals are intentionally simple and don't take a lot of time. And, did I mention that they're extremely effective?*

After you've committed to making feeling good your highest priority and using the two Daily Tools, if it strikes you that you'd love to create a vision board or that you'd like to spend more time visualizing your goals, great! By committing to these two Daily Tools, however, tools that can be effective for nearly everyone, you can relax and know that your work is done. Anything else you might do to improve your vibration can be considered icing on the cake.

Rather than feeling scattered or confused about whether you've actually practiced maintaining your positive vibration, you can know that you've done what you need to do. Anything else you might do because it's fun or comes naturally to you is a bonus. And, of course, having that relaxed feeling that you've done your work, honored your commitment, is, in itself, contributing to a higher vibration!

So, I hope I've convinced you to consider a commitment to two Daily Tools, one of which I'll introduce in this lesson. The second tool I'll focus on in the next lesson. Now, I'd like to explain clearly exactly why this first Tool is so effective and how such fantastic results have been achieved by me and so many others. It will help you to understand the mindset you'll be trying to create as part of the first Tool.

First, I'd like to go over a couple of the other processes I've mentioned, which *can* work beautifully but often don't work for many people; it will help you to understand how you can use the spirit of those processes as part of this Tool, while avoiding their potential pitfalls. When, in my excitement, I first began to share my knowledge of the Law of Attraction with others, I saw that individual tools I'd share could sometimes achieve immediate positive results. Usually, however, these results were very temporary.

In the case of a friend I'll call Tom, who was being seriously challenged by health issues, anxiety and depression, I suggested that he spend just a few minutes each day writing down the positive aspects of the things that were important in his life. This technique that I learned from the spiritual teachers known as Abraham can bring quick, positive results. Tom was somewhat skeptical, I could tell, but he was feeling so desperate that he made an attempt to follow my advice for a brief time.

I suggested that he take a notebook and at the top of each page write the name of a person or situation in his life and to list beneath it as many positive things about that person or area of his life that he could come up with. I reminded him that, despite his health issues, he had a wonderful wife that was devoted to him, two great kids, parents who loved him, a secure high-paying job. I suggested that by sitting down and focusing on those things for just a few minutes each day, he could begin to raise his vibration and improve not only those things in his life, but his health as well.

After a couple of weeks, I checked in to see how

he was doing and he responded that he had just decided, on a whim, to buy a sports car he had always wanted. He had compromised on his own car for years so that his teenagers could have reliable cars. His voice had a wholly different tone. He was excited, had taken the day off work, and his college-age son was meeting him that afternoon to take a maiden voyage in the new sports car. He even found himself saying to me, "It doesn't get much better than this, meeting my son to take our first drive in my new sports car." Even I was amazed at the dramatic and rapid improvement in his outlook and how he was spending his day after such a relatively short period of time. Prior to that, I hadn't heard him speak of anything remotely positive in his experience as he was so focused on his continuing health issues; he had been experiencing physical pain, severe anxiety and had been unable to work on most days.

Tom, being the skeptic that he was, still didn't quite appreciate the connection between that few minutes he was spending each day appreciating the good things in his life and the positive momentum he was experiencing. While I'd like to say that Tom's health improved and his life went into an upward trajectory, he didn't continue with the practice of focusing each day on the positive aspects of his life. He wasn't a big believer in the Law of Attraction, and it would be three more years of continuing health issues before he made any significant progress with his health or anxiety problems.

While it may seem remarkable, in the case of Tom,

that simply spending a few minutes a day focusing on the positive aspects of his life resulted in such a quick shift in his momentum, remember how much more powerful positively vibrating energy is in comparison to murky, fragmented energy. Because higher vibrating energy is exponentially more powerful that negatively vibrating energy, it's not necessary that you replace twenty years of negative thinking with twenty years of appreciation in order to raise your vibration. Your vibration can begin to shift immediately by your decision to think the best thoughts of which you're capable in this moment.

Another factor which can cause such quick results in the case of someone who has been experiencing significant challenges or contrast, is that their continued sending out of their desire for improvement has resulted in the amassing of a huge stockpile in their vibrational reality. They've been asking and asking for improvement, and Source Energy has been responding continually. What they've created in terms of their vibrational escrow is huge! Even a small positive shift in their focus and hence, their vibration, can provide such relief for them that it can yield almost immediate evidence of improvement.

Several years ago, an old high school friend I'll call Julie had a similar experience to Tom in terms of seeing an almost immediate response to the shifting of her vibration. She had been experiencing long-standing problems in her marriage and had nearly given up on keeping her marriage intact. She was new to the Law of

Attraction and had some pretty healthy skepticism. She had seen some of the results in my life, however, and was interested in anything that might help. I suggested that she try to focus on the best aspects of her husband and that those aspects would begin to show up for her more frequently because she would be attracting what she was focused upon.

She had been so disappointed in her husband's attitude that she had been nearly constantly focused on what he was doing wrong. Her emotional state was in the range of hopelessness, anger and frustration. Because, in her view, her husband had done little in recent days to focus positively upon, I suggested that she take a few minutes each day picturing her husband as he was when they first began dating. I asked her to remember some of the really quite nice things he had done for her over the years. We also talked about imagining him responding more positively during some of their interactions that ordinarily would have resulted in confrontation.

When I spoke to her within just a week, she reported that her husband had approached her with an apology about the way he had been behaving and told her he was committed to making things better between them. I think Julie was in shock! She hadn't communicated anything to him verbally, only through her focus on his positive aspects. Again, however, as in the case of Tom, Julie continued to approach the issue in an inconsistent way. She would try to focus positively on her husband whenever she thought of it or could bring herself to do it. Her problems with her spouse continued for quite some time without any real commitment on her part to raise her vibration.

My enthusiasm over the rapid positive results that would follow from even modest efforts, coupled with my strong desire for more consistent results, led to the development of this practical system. I've seen that, without a commitment to some daily consistent practice, and the decision to make maintaining your vibration your highest priority, the results can be only temporary and erratic.

> *A daily practice and a real commitment to raising your vibration, are essential to making more fundamental changes in the circumstances of your life. And, that's exactly what the two Daily Tools are all about.*

How the Process for Tuning Up Your Vibration Works

Put very simply, things first began to really break loose in my life when I began using this technique. I had been able to manifest some positive changes in my life, up to that point, but the results were, at best, sporadic and unpredictable. It is hard to convey how hard I tried to think positively, monitor my thoughts and visualize positive outcomes to undesirable circumstances.

You may be thinking you know exactly how I felt. While thinking more positively about your current experiences works to the extent that you are able to do it, it seems almost impossible to think predominantly positive thoughts when surrounded by difficult circumstances such as a painful relationship, severe financial pressures or health issues. It can seem almost unimaginable to create positive momentum because, in the midst of very trying circumstances, it is almost impossible not to focus a fair amount of time on the difficulty.

> *This is because most of us have been trained to focus on any problem area in our lives and to take action to fix the problem so that we can then be happy. And, of course, knowing what you now know about the Law of Attraction, focusing on your problems is a certain way to both perpetuate the problems and attract similarly vibrating problems!*

In my own quest to think positively, I tried using **affirmations**, which can be effective, but often are not. Affirmations are positive statements of what we want to create in our lives, repeated frequently throughout the day, as a way of creating the expectation that we will achieve those desires. An example of an affirmation for someone wanting to improve his or her financial situation would be "I am financially successful," or "I am rich and money comes easily to me." The problem with affirmations such as these, however, is that most people, while repeating, "I am financially successful," are actually thinking, "Yeah, right."

> *There must be a basic underlying belief and positive expectation that the goal is achievable in order to generate the positive vibration necessary to make the affirmation effective.*

And, for most people, the vibration surrounding the desire expressed in the affirmation is really quite mixed. You've created the affirmative statement of what you want **precisely because you don't yet have it**. Without any effort at raising your vibration prior to using the affirmation, or a sincere belief in its viability, the affirmation isn't generating the necessary positive vibe to attract what you want. In fact, it's only reinforcing a negative focus on not having enough money.

> *Remember that the Universe isn't responding to the words we use but only our underlying vibration.*

So repeating frequently throughout the day that, "I have a healthy and fit body," when you're twenty pounds overweight and discouraged, really only serves to reinforce your expectation that you'll continue to be twenty pounds overweight. There are, however, ways to make using positive statements of our desires more effective, which I'll discuss as part of this Daily Tool.

In addition to using affirmations in my quest to learn to Allow, I also tried **visualization**, the concept first made popular by author Shakti Gawain in her book *Creative Visualization*. Visualization is a process, like affirmations, which can work amazingly well when used effectively, but can prove difficult for many people. In the past, when I tried to visualize my desires, I found it too easy to let my mind wander. I also found it hard to concentrate on my desired scenario for more than a few moments before my thoughts gravitated toward the problem I was hoping to visualize my way out of.

Many report similar problems with visualizing. Other people have trouble because they think they aren't creative or don't have the ability to imagine the circumstances they'd like to create. Like any of the other means used to try to raise your vibration, if visualization is used solely in a hit or miss fashion only when we remember to focus, it is difficult to achieve any consistent raising of our vibration.

You will see, however, that the ability to create effectively through visualization can be developed through practice and through the use of the First Daily Tool introduced in this Lesson.

As a result of learning and trying these processes as well as others, including the notebook of positive aspects mentioned earlier, I learned what did and didn't work and began to understand why. Positive thoughts, intentions, and mental visions all are essential to the process of deliberate creation, but must actually generate a positive vibration and be used on a consistent basis in order to be effective.

I found that I could generate that positive vibe on a more consistent basis through using the first Daily Tool, Tuning Up Your Vibration. It is a daily ritual that incorporates some of the best aspects of a variety of other tools in a way that helps you to actually raise your vibration as you do the process. It also helps you to maintain that higher vibration for a reasonable period of time.

As you might imagine, your mindset in using this process is most important. Everything, after all, is a mental game as our thoughts and the feelings they generate do all of our creating. In the following section we'll nail down exactly the mindset we'll be working to achieve in doing the Tuning up Process.

Understanding the Goal of the Tuning Up Process

Before trying the first Daily Tool, let's get into the right frame of mind about where we are and where we are hoping to be by the end of the process. First, it is important to acknowledge that while it is good to focus positively on our desires as often as we can, it is impossible to completely control our thoughts. And, once we've begun to focus on a problem in our lives, our thoughts often begin to spiral in that direction, seemingly out of our control.

We can let ourselves off of the hook for that tendency, however, when we understand that our thoughts are real energy, and that those negative thoughts go out into the ethers to magnetically attract similar negative thoughts. That's why it's easy to pick up momentum in a negative direction. It is as if your mind gets into a loop of negative thoughts from which it's hard to disengage. Rather than beating yourself up for your current emotional state, remind yourself that recognizing negative emotion is something to be proud of; it means you're becoming more aware of your emotional guidance system, your communication from Source that you're out of alignment with your desires.

> *Negative emotion simply means that you're not viewing the situation from the perspective of Source. And, it's fully within your power to change your thoughts to those that feel a little bit better in that moment.*

It is important that you have the mindset, as we embark on the use of the Daily Tune up, that:

Where I am in my present circumstances and my mood at this moment is temporary, and can be changed now. And, wherever I am is okay. I'm happy that I'm aware of the guidance provided by my emotions. I know now how the laws work. I know that I have the ability to shift my mood at any time to come into alignment with my desires. And, when I've done that, I can relax in the knowing that what I desire is on its way to me. I intend to make the best of everything.

I'm going to suggest that you paste the paragraph above or a similar one that resonates with you at the beginning of the page where you begin your Daily Tune-up so that it helps to set the tone for your writing. It could be pasted on the top of your computer or a template could be created in your document, or you could put it on a card to read through before you begin writing by hand. This sentiment, or something like it, will help you to begin the process with the kind of mindset that can help you to get a great start on tuning up your vibration.

Tuning Up Your Vibration—The Process!!

The Daily Tune up will involve writing, either by hand or on your computer for a short period of time each day, perhaps ten or fifteen minutes or whatever feels comfortable for you, in what will usually be a three-step process. I've learned that writing is one of the most powerful ways we have of maintaining our focus. There is a certain magic that comes into play when we engage in writing about our desires. While we're engaged in writing, we're **affirming our intention, focusing on our desired outcome, and bringing more clarity to our desires.**

This powerful daily tool *will not* be journaling for the purpose of venting or letting go of thoughts and concerns, although it could have the effect of releasing your fixation on any problems in your life. It is rather, directed, focused writing for the purpose of:

(1) making peace with your current circumstances and letting go of as much resistant thought as you can;

(2) developing a feeling of appreciation about where you are and faith about where you are heading; and

(3) writing about things as you'd like them to be as if they've already come into being.

> *This process could be summed up as working through layers of your thinking on the various aspects of your life until you're actually expecting beyond what currently "is." This activity gets you into the state of feeling as if your desire has manifested before you've seen any evidence of it, which is the real secret to deliberate creation!*

This three-step process, by beginning in Step 1 with making peace with your current circumstances, avoids the possible problematic aspect of writing about something as you wish it to be when you're negatively focused on your current circumstances. When you begin writing an affirmation or writing about something as you want it to be from a state of negative or mixed vibration, you often aren't able to arrive in the state of positive vibration or expectation that needs to accompany the statement in order for it to be effective.

So in *Step 1* you're going to talk yourself into a better feeling state about where you are right now by writing about things as they are, while finding ways of thinking about your circumstances that feel better than your usual thoughts.

> *Particularly if something is bothering you, this will be the Step in which you'll find a better way of viewing the situation and move into feeling that everything is okay now as it is. It is a temporary point at which you've arrived and you can go anywhere from here.*

Similarly, Step 2 of the daily writing process, moving beyond just making peace with your current situation to finding a real feeling of appreciation for the things you currently have in your life, avoids the difficulty most people have with just sitting down and beginning to imagine their desired outcome. Starting from ground zero, with whatever may have been going on in your current thoughts, can make it difficult to concentrate for more than a few moments, or to even conjure up thoughts and images which are vibrating far from where you are. You're only able to access thoughts that are reasonably close to where you're currently vibrating.

For example, your fight with your significant other makes you want to improve your relationship. When you begin to write about or visualize a better relationship you will likely find it nearly impossible to launch immediately into writing about the two of you smiling and enjoying each other's company. Even if you are able to create that image of an improved relationship in your imagination, you are likely to lose your concentration and find yourself back in the state of remembering how your significant other was aloof or distant before they left for work. It can be really hard to maintain that ideal vision when you begin without working yourself into a higher state of vibration.

So, in Step 2 you're going to be moving right into writing lightly, easily, about the things you have in your life right now that you appreciate. They don't have to be "big." They could or might not be about your significant other, in this case. They can be small things you appreciate about your life, your day, or the things that happened for you yesterday. You'll write about whatever comes into your head that's worthy of appreciation as you create an even better feeling vibration.

Finally, Step 3 of this process brings in the tool often referred to as "scripting" or writing about things as if they already are as you actually want them to be.

By working your way up to this step by gradually raising your vibration, you are able to avoid the problem many people have with scripting. While scripting can be a fantastic tool and can operate to create seeming miracles, most people find it hard to jump into writing about their desired reality in the present tense, as if it's real, without any sort of groundwork. This process for Tuning up Your Vibration, however, gradually moves your thoughts to a higher state of vibration. This allows you to make the leap to writing about things as you would like them to be as if they're already true, while actually having the good feelings that these outcomes would generate.

> *The things you're asking for are already true, by the way, and being held in perfect readiness by the Universe in your vibrational reality. This process will help you to move to the place where you've generated the positive emotion that will allow you to really believe in the outcome you're scripting.*

This Step 3 of the process, which I've described as writing about your desires as if they've already materialized, has sometimes been associated with the concept of "praying rain." This term of art comes from author Gregg Braden's story about a Native American friend who took him to a remote desert site for the purpose of creating rain during a long drought in New Mexico.

In a nutshell, Gregg's Native American friend, rather than chanting and dancing and praying for rain, instead spent a few moments of quiet and then remarked that he was finished. Braden's friend explained that if he prayed "for" rain he wouldn't get rain because he would be focusing on the very condition he didn't want, the absence of rain. Instead, he "prayed rain," by feeling the rain falling on his body, smelling it in the air and tasting it on his tongue, and imagining the crops growing wildly due to all that rain that was falling. As you can imagine, it did rain, and rained a lot! For a great take on praying rain, in general, Law of Attraction coach extraordinaire, Jeannette Maw, has written an e-book called *The Magic of Pray Rain Journaling* at www.prayrainjournaling.com (See Recommended Resources Section for more information.)

So, in the all-important Step 3 of the Daily Tune-up, you're going to be writing about your desire(s) as if they've already manifested for you, creating the tingles in your body that you'd have if those desires were already a reality. Think of it as writing a movie script, with you as the star, filling in all of the details, as you'd like them to be. It's fun, feels really good, and puts you right into that state of positive vibration that is an exact match to the things you've been wanting.

The good news is that you will naturally move into visualizing your desired outcome as you go through the Daily Tune-up because you won't be starting from whatever random vibration you may have had going. You will have gradually worked yourself into the state of higher vibration that will allow you to think about your desire while maintaining a vibration that matches it. And, a bonus of this process is that you are practicing visualizing your dreams every day, gradually, until it does become easier to visualize, in general, even when you're not doing the Daily Tune-up Process. While I used to have difficulty visualizing my goals in my head and remaining focused, after using this process for awhile, I found that it became easier and easier to imagine things as I'd like them to be at any time.

As I was writing this section, I experienced a perfect example of the power of doing this exercise, especially before taking any action to resolve an issue or problem. I had ordered some prescription medications for one of my dogs from an online prescription service, which is quicker and more reasonable than getting the prescriptions from the veterinarian. The online company keeps a record of all of your pet's information and your veterinarian, and contacts your vet to refill the prescription before mailing it to you. I'd had a few snags with our new veterinarian, which consists of a large group of doctors. Sometimes it has taken as long as a week to get an authorization or they've asked me to bring my dog in for a blood test before they will authorize the prescription. This was true even though I'd previously brought my dog in for a complete checkup, including blood tests, so that I could get her prescriptions when she needed them. So, to avoid any more issues, I had made sure that all of my dog's tests were up to date and that her prescriptions were valid. I even spoke to the vet who had treated her when I had problems ordering prescriptions before and mentioned my concerns. It had been frustrating that I had spent the time and money to get my dog a blood test, and yet they would still find a reason to deny the prescription.

So, with everything in order this time, I ordered the prescriptions and received an e-mail from the company that one prescription would be filled but that the veterinarian insisted that I come in to the vet's office to get the other prescription. I was definitely annoyed and the initial thoughts I had were along the lines of, "they want to make it difficult so that people will buy their more expensive prescriptions; they want me to come in and order expensive blood work even though I've already brought my dog in, and they're just trying to make it a hassle so that people will give up on the online service and they can make more of a profit." This line of thought, while possibly accurate, was definitely not conducive to things going my way.

So, instead of calling the vet and complaining, which was my first instinct, I put it on my to do list and did nothing. Then when I did my Daily Tune-Up, I wrote about how good the online pharmacy was and how the vet group is actually very competent too. They **are** trying to provide good care for my pets. They are so busy and the group is so large that it would be easy for someone to make a mistake. And, the last time this happened, they did relent and allowed me to get my prescription. I talked myself down some more until the issue just didn't have any charge for me.
I

I went from being angry, frustrated that they were trying to take advantage of patients, to feeling like I'm glad that I have a good veterinarian as well as the online service and I know everything will work out. I planned to call the vet when I got a chance and ask that they authorize the prescription, but, two days later, before I did anything, I received an e-mail from the online company that the other medication had been shipped. Weird, huh? First, it wasn't authorized. In fact, they had insisted that I come in to get the prescription. Yet, I had taken no action other than writing about it and now it was on its way to me. The Tune-Up process really works! The writing exercise really focuses your attention and allows you to gradually change your vibration to one that not only feels much better, but will give you much better outcomes.

Before giving you the opportunity to try the Daily Tune-Up, I'd like to give some examples of how it might work for you, and then focus on why the process would operate to raise your vibration and Allow in your desires.

The writing process for the Daily Tune-up should be easy, and should always improve your mood! You don't need to be concerned with grammar, or pleasing anyone else with what you've written. Ideally, it should be something you can do in private and without interruption so that you can feel free to write whatever would generate positive feelings for you without regard to how anyone else might feel or how "realistic" your writing is. **It's not supposed to be realistic!** When I was writing about the veterinarian approving my prescription easily, I knew that it contradicted the reality of the e-mail I had just received, but I know that it's okay to ignore reality and write about things as I want them to be.

Remember, the process is not meant to involve venting in order to purge negative emotion. That being said, sometimes it might be necessary to begin with a brief focus on something that is bothering you if you're preoccupied with that issue. That was the case for me on the day I had the hassle of my prescription being denied. Then you'll use your writing process to come up with better feeling thoughts on that issue. This all really depends, of course, on where you are each day when you begin the process.

Below is an example of one person's writing when they were feeling some concern about a family member, but also wanted to focus on creating a better work situation for themselves.

Step 1 (Making Peace with Where You Are Right Now):

When I woke up this morning, I briefly had that nagging, worried feeling. I was focusing bon the fact that Andrew seems to be slipping a bit in school again. I've felt that bway before, though, and things have always turned out okay. I know that worrying about it isn't going to improve the situation, for me or for Andrew. Actually, I know it's silly to worry. He's a great kid, very smart and he always gets it together eventually. He's learning a lot now about how to be more organized and he's doing so much better than he did in the past at being more responsible about his schoolwork. This is just a blip, I know, and I could give him a little gentle encouragement to keep trying to do his best. I really do trust his judgment and that he knows the right thing to do. And, he's learning from his mistakes and these aren't really big ones.

Step 2 (Flowing Appreciation for Other Aspects of Your Life):

All in all, I have so much to appreciate about my family, how well my kids are doing. They're all such funny, kind, intelligent, compassionate people. They know how to follow their own guidance. They could teach me a few things! I know I can be a powerful influence on them when I focus on all of their best qualities.

It's great to have such a wonderful family and such close relationships with each other. I do appreciate how my kids thank me for nearly everything I do for them. I must have raised them well. And, my husband is getting better and better about showing his appreciation too. I'm really pretty lucky in that regard. It was so nice of him to bring me flowers last week. He really works hard at being a good husband and father and he understands me like no one else.

I'm intending to find more and more positive aspects of my work as well. While I'd really like to make a change and find something that gives me more flexibility, I am recognized for my contributions there. I have good friends at work that make my life more fun every day. And, I do have some flexibility in my schedule when I really need it.

Step 3 (Scripting or Writing About What You Want As If It Already "IS":

My employer surely would allow me a bit more flexibility, perhaps to work a couple of days per week from home. That does feel great. I enjoy having some time at home in the afternoon with the kids before dinner. I'm more relaxed, having gotten a few things taken care of at home when I took a break from working. Without my commute, I have time to walk the dog more often, getting a bit more exercise, which I enjoy. I think our dinners are improving now that I have more energy! I think I'm even bringing more creativity to work with this sort of schedule.

I think they probably feel that I'm due for a raise. I do appreciate their flexibility at work and how much they value me.

For now, the improvement in my mood is all the evidence I need that positive changes are on their way to me. I know that when I line up my energy like this, what I want is on its way.

In this example, this woman has gradually worked herself into being able to script out an improved work situation for herself while she maintains a feeling of appreciation. As she began the process, she was negatively focused on a problem with one of her kids. That preoccupation would have prevented her from launching immediately into a positive script or visualization about her work while maintaining a state of positive expectation. She needed to gently deal with her slight worry about her son and then move into a state of appreciation about the things that were working in her life. Then, from there, she was able to easily visualize and write the script of a more flexible schedule and how it would feel to have that improved situation. And, this simple process can be applied to any situation from wherever you are.

On another day, you might find yourself in a fairly good mood, having mostly positive expectations. In that case, you could move fairly quickly through making peace with where you are into really ramping up your appreciation for what you already have in your life. When you've been able to do that fairly easily, it's often simple to script out your perfect scenario to match one of your desires while maintaining feelings of pure positive emotion:

Step 1 (Making Peace with Where You Are)

Wow, it was so great to wake up this morning and be so excited about my work! It's taken me awhile but I'm so glad that I've developed this clarity about the direction of my writing. I know that I caused myself to arrive at this place by focusing on my desire to create this project and I'm proud of myself. Although there is much more to do, I'm so happy to be at this juncture with tons of ideas and inspiration and a real vision.

Step 2 (Flowing Appreciation for Things That Are Working)

There are so many things that seem to be going well for me and I know that it carries over into my writing. I'm glad that I re-connected with two friends who I missed and it's been great to share my ideas with them again. It's so fun to share my inspiration with my spouse. I know my enthusiasm is contagious. There are so many things to appreciate right now. I love our family dinners and our Friday pizza nights. I love it that the kids are off from school and we have more time together. I love it that everyone is having so much fun with our new puppy. I love it that I live close enough to my mom to have lunch with her every week. My life feels balanced.

Step 3 (Scripting or Writing About Your Desires As If They Already "Are"):

In fact, I'm feeling so good about the way this writing is going and I see so many people appreciating it that I know I could help thousands of people with this project. I can hardly believe the testimonials I'm getting from the people I've worked with. I love doing this work and I love helping people. I really love this flexible schedule and how it allows me time to do work I love while still enjoying my family and my hobbies.

Hey, I could see myself on Oprah! The financial windfall is better than I even imagined. The whole family really appreciates what I'm doing and is proud of me! I'm planning a family trip to Asia, which I've wanted to do for so long. And, I think I'll get a new couch for our living room. I love making our house look fantastic. I'd like to do some landscaping too. I'll get out some garden catalogs and get some good ideas. Sitting out on our new patio with beautiful plantings around it is so much fun. It's such a sanctuary. I love inviting friends over for dinner to take in the setting.

This person has worked herself into a great state of positive expectation. I'm cutting into this incomplete example to make an important point, however. During this Tuning Up Process, it's important to focus on your ideal situation in only enough detail that it feels good. In the example above, if the writer began to envision doing some elaborate renovation of her house with her financial windfall and starting to feel the mixed feeling of (ugh, renovation is so difficult), it would be better not to jump into the idea of renovation. It would be better to keep her ideas about improving her home more general or on a smaller scale where it was easy to maintain excitement.

Alternatively, were this same writer to continue to talk about buying a new car, it might continue to generate that tingling feeling of positive anticipation. However, this same writer, if they continued into writing about building their dream vacation home, might begin to feel that she was getting too far from where she could generate real belief and expectation. It would really depend, of course, on the attitude of the creator. You need to be the judge of how much detail to go into when you begin to describe things the way you want them to be. If you begin to write about something you want but you start to go a bit limp, it's time to pull back and focus on a more general picture of you happily enjoying yourself in only as much detail as creates that feeling of positive expectation.

There should be no limit on the amount you write on a particular day. I generally keep writing until I've really gotten myself into my vortex of creation, that pure positive state which matches my desires. Then, I try to maintain that state for a while with my writing. You might find yourself writing quite a bit more than the examples I've given. In the exercises that follow, you'll get a chance to try this process for yourself while I continue to reinforce the effect you're trying to create. You really can't get this wrong but it's helpful to have a sense of where you'd like to end up each day as you do the process.

Lesson Four Practice (Part A)

Before asking that you try the Daily Tool for tuning up your vibration, I'd like to focus like a laser on what we're trying to achieve as a result of this writing process so that the steps make absolute sense. After all, this process will be unique to you and will depend on where you find yourself on a given day and what you intend to accomplish. In some cases for your Step 3, scripting, you might need to write around your desire rather than focusing on it head on. You may not be able to write about your desire as if it's occurred with real conviction the first few times you attempt it. This will be your creativity at work, with the goal of getting yourself where you can write about your desires as if you've already achieved them while in a state of pure positive emotion!

Remember that Allowing is, in its most simple form, raising your vibration in any way you can to get yourself into your vibrational vortex with your desire. One way to get clear on the vibration you're trying to match is to determine the vibrational essence of your desire. The vibrational essence of your desire is it's basic nature, what your desire means to you. It's how you think achieving the desire will make you feel. For example, if your goal were financial security or enough money to pay your bills easily, the feelings that might result from attracting financial abundance might be feelings of security, independence, freedom, peace or even power, depending upon your unique situation. If your desire was to improve a relationship or find a new relationship, the feelings that might result from that relationship could be security, love or excitement. In either case, the feelings you're trying to generate in your writing process are those same feelings; feelings of security, freedom, independence, or however you think your desire will make you feel.

So, you could approach achieving the feelings that match having your desire in one of two ways: you could imagine it already having happened, thereby creating the feeling while you're imagining it; or, you can search for things you already have in your life that evoke those same feelings and focus upon them. Does that make sense because it's a very important way of thinking about Allowing in your desires?

In the case of financial security, that first approach would mean writing a story about yourself as financially successful, paying your bills easily, buying things you want, taking trips, whatever financial security would mean to you. The alternate approach would be to write about those other things in your life that already cause you to feel security or freedom, for example, your relationship with your spouse might cause you to feel secure. Your part-time job could allow you a flexible schedule and give you feelings of independence. You would want to spend time focusing on those positive aspects of your marriage or your job and how appreciative you are of those feelings of security and independence they give you.

The second approach, finding things to appreciate that you already have which match the feelings of your desire, might be thought of as getting into your vibrational escrow by way of the back door. This can be helpful when you've got so much negative expectation surrounding your desire, in this case, financial security, that it's just too difficult to write about having financial security as if it already exists while maintaining pure positive feelings. It may just feel too unrealistic at first.

When you're having difficulty scripting out your desire as if it's already happened because there is too much negative emotion surrounding the subject, your Step 3 instead would involve writing specifically about things that generate the same positive emotions as the essence of your desire.

With either approach, you're raising your vibration to match the essence of what you're hoping to achieve by having financial security and shifting the momentum of your vibration so that financial security is on its way to you. You're letting it in.

As a preliminary step before taking a shot at the Daily Tune-Up, I'd like for you to refer back to your list of intentions from Lesson Two, where you were also asked to indicate why you wanted those things in your life. Make a list of the desires you'd like to focus upon, at this point, and for each of them list the essence of that desire, how you think having that desire will make you feel. Then, as you go through the three steps of the Daily Tune-up you'll be mindful of the types of feelings you're trying to generate.

Desires to Focus Upon:

Essence of the Desires:

This process is, of necessity, malleable and adaptable to wherever you find yourself on a given day. In the following example the writer is facing serious financial hardship and is finding it difficult not to focus on the state of his bank balance. In this case, the path of least resistance would be to make peace with where he is, in general, by focusing on the good things in his life and try to get into a state of appreciation of those things that match the essence of financial security. It might not be possible for him to visualize a financial windfall while starting from such a place of insecurity. It might take a few days of writing or more to work himself into a state where he could write a script about having all of the money he needs to pay his bills easily while feeling the buzz of positive emotion.

> *I began the day today checking my e-mails and found myself focusing on my online bank account. Ugh, when will this end? I know I need to focus beyond "what is" right now and I'm doing my best to do that. I have made feeling good my highest priority and I know that focusing on the bank balance is not honoring that commitment to feeling good. There are so many positives in my life to focus upon. When I checked my e-mail I had notes from three good friends and from my dad. I'm so lucky to have so many people who care about me. And, I know I could rely on help from any of them if I really needed it. I'm healthy, and I do have work, which is helping to*

pay some of our bills.

I need to remind myself of how lucky I am really. It was so much fun to see our old friends this weekend and to be able to pick up right where we left off. I really appreciate having good friends and family so near. There are so many things we can do which don't rely on having a tremendous amount of money. Watching movies with our family is one of my favorite activities, and costs virtually nothing. And, we always have good food in our house and manage to find fun activities to enjoy together. I do have a great deal of freedom really. I am mostly able to do just what I want to do. And that's a good thing. I'm lucky to have such a good marriage, a wife I can rely on, who always appreciates me. The support system I have, my wife, my many friends and extended family, do give me a feeling of security. And, now I know as I didn't before how the laws of the Universe work. I know that, at any moment, I can change my thoughts to match the vibration of my desire. And, I know that when I do, things must change. So, for now, I'm appreciating all of the good things I have, the knowledge I have, and the good things that are on their way to me when I take the time to line up my energy. I know they're on their way.

There is another possible approach that I'd like to suggest when there is a "big issue" which seems impossible to tackle head on in terms of creating a believable fantasy of your ideal scenario. You would still, of course, want to go through the Step 1 process of making peace with where you are as best you could. You would also go onto Step 2 of generating more appreciation for the things you have in your life right now. When it comes to the Step 3, or writing about the improved condition as if it's already occurred, you could take a slightly different approach.

This approach can be especially helpful when the "big issue" is financial prosperity where many people find it hard to visualize beyond their depleted bank account. They begin to think about how and when the money will get there and find it hard to really expect the big improvement. Mike Dooley, a fabulous speaker and writer on deliberate creation, calls the preoccupation with how things will manifest the "cursed how's." It is worth reading his take on this issue in his book, *Infinite Possibilities,* referred to in the Recommended Resources.

During the writing process, instead, for Step 3 you could just make a list of all of the things you would do if money were no object at all. Making this list avoids the potential focus on "how and when" and moves you right into focusing on the positive feelings. You can ratchet up your positive feelings even more by taking your list a step further and writing down how you'd feel if you were doing each thing on your list.

Here's an example of how that might work:

If money were no issue at all I would: pay off all of my credit cards (woo): take my daughter on a shopping spree for new clothes; treat my best friend to lunch; donate to our local animal shelter; hire a housekeeper; buy some new casual clothes; join a health club; book a cruise with my spouse for our anniversary; treat my parents to a vacation; get new furniture for my office; make some fun investments. Wow, paying off my credit cards would make me feel free, unencumbered, proud of myself. Taking my daughter shopping would make me feel even more like a great, generous parent; Hiring a housekeeper would make me feel free, like I had more time for things I like to do.

Making the list alone is a great way of generating that positive buzz you're trying to create if it might be a bit difficult to write about your life as if you already have all of the financial abundance you want. After using this approach for some time, you'd likely be able to work up to writing a script about your financial prosperity as if it's already happened while maintaining that buzz of positive emotion.

While generally you'll be able to dive into Tuning Up your Vibration by going through the three steps of making peace with where you are, appreciating things in your life that are working and finally, scripting out your perfect scenario, each day may be different, depending upon where you find yourself in terms of your emotions. The goal is to eventually get to writing about your desire as if it's already manifested while having pure positive emotion and belief in your desired outcome. You will need to be the judge of how to get there from where you are, whether by writing about or around your dreams until you can generate the pure vibration of your desire.

Lesson Four Practice (Part B)

Okay, now take some time to try Tuning Up Your Vibration. And commit to making it a daily or nearly daily practice. I would try to insist on making it a daily practice but I understand that there may be occasional days when you really don't have the privacy or flexibility to do the process. These days should be rare, though. I've found that when I've missed doing the process, I can see the results in what is going on around me. What I should say is that when I do the process, I can really see the positive results in what is going on around me. I have also found that it gets easier and easier to do and to get quickly into scripting out your ideal scenario. It begins to feel so good to do it that you look forward to it. And, once you start seeing the results of your efforts, you begin to look forward to it even more.

Make it work in a way that's best for you, keeping in mind what you're trying to achieve. Make peace with where you are, ramp up your appreciation for what already is, and finally, write about your desire as if it's already a done deal!

Tuning Up Your Vibration:

Lesson Five: The Second Daily Tool—Going Within and Releasing Resistance

As you begin to make Tuning Up Your Vibration a ritual that you practice consistently, you should begin to see some solid evidence of the shifting of your vibration. Some good things that you've been resisting up until now should begin to show themselves to you. If you haven't yet begun to see evidence of small positive changes in your circumstances, remember that when you are doing the work, the things you desire are on their way to you.

When things I've been wanting have not yet begun to show themselves, I like to remind myself that my "mood" really is my early evidence of the attraction of my desires. That's really all the evidence I need because I know that when I ask, my request is responded to by Source and my improved mood is evidence of my alignment with what Source is creating for me. It's just the way the laws work. Nonetheless, I would expect you to see some immediate evidence of the beginnings of good things coming into your life fairly soon after beginning to use this daily ritual.

I did say, however, that I consider there to be two pivotal tools in learning How to Allow. The tool to be introduced in this section is equally important as it has two very important effects that help to support you in writing the new story of your life during the Tune-Up Process. This second Daily Tool is meditation or quieting your mind briefly each day; I'm hoping you didn't groan when you read the word meditation. For lots of people, the word meditation conjures up difficult poses, mantras, chanting, and trying to keep your mind free of any thoughts, which seems absolutely impossible.

I'd like to be clear from the outset, though, that what I have in mind, which has worked for many, is a very simple approach to allowing the mind to relax from it's usual focus on constant thoughts. It doesn't require years of study or practice. Although, I have noticed that it becomes much easier after a fairly short period. All that is required is the devotion of about fifteen or twenty minutes a day to relaxing, with the intent of quieting the mind, or letting go of the constant stream of resistant thoughts most of us have.

Before talking about how to do this process as simply as possible, I'd like to make sure that you fully appreciate the two profound benefits of meditation which will support your ability to Allow your Well-Being. When you are able to relax and let go of most of the random thoughts that dart through your mind, you enter a resistance-free state that is a vibrational match to your desires. Even if you are only in the resistance-free state for ten minutes of your twenty-minute meditation each day, you've lined up with Source Energy and have begun Allowing in the things you've asked for.

> *Remember, that pure positive energy is exponentially more powerful than negative or mixed energy. Ten minutes each day, awake and free of resistance, can go a long way toward raising your vibrational set point, that is, the vibration you generally gravitate toward.*

The second important effect of meditation, is that it also creates a greater sensitivity to negative emotion or being out of alignment. The process of meditation, because it creates the feeling of being aligned with Source Energy, allows you to recognize negative emotion at an earlier, subtler, state, when it is much easier to make a correction.

We've learned that Allowing is really about being constantly tuned into your emotional guidance system, recognizing your emotional state and using your focus to improve it whenever you notice negative emotion. And, meditation is just the tool for tuning up your sensitivity to negative emotion so that it becomes something you're less likely to tolerate. Meditation really supports your commitment to making feeling good your highest priority.

The other good news about meditation is that once you give it a chance, it will become something you look forward to each day. It can provide instant relief from any resistance you may be experiencing, and can be especially helpful when you're finding it difficult to choose better feeling thoughts when something is really bothering you.

While there are myriad books and CD's describing different methods of meditation, the process really can be as simple as you'd like it to be. I recommend trying to keep it simple; see for yourself how easy it can be and how quickly you can benefit from this basic practice. Later, you can always choose to try some of the other meditative practices that are out there, such as guided meditations, if you think you might enjoy them.

To meditate or quiet your mind it's really only necessary to allow about fifteen or twenty minutes each day where you won't be interrupted. It's considered helpful to meditate at roughly the same time each day as your body and mind become accustomed to the practice and begin to line up with your positive expectation of relaxation. That said, I firmly believe in not imposing lots of requirements on these tools, which can make you feel as if you're not doing enough or doing it right. So, with meditation, as with the other parts of this course, the point is to keep it simple and flexible and that you feel good while doing it. If you can meditate at the same time each day, that's great, but if you can't, not a big deal. The big deal is to commit to your two Daily Tools. The rituals will help you to avoid the problems of consistency that most people have with harnessing the power of the Universe to achieve their desires.

In order to meditate, it is best to sit in a comfortable position, even lying down if you won't fall asleep, with your eyes closed. It helps to relax your muscles as you begin. It can be good to move through each muscle group, briefly tensing and relaxing the muscles until your entire body feels relaxed. Prior to letting go of your thoughts, it can be good to mentally affirm your intention for your meditation. Your intention as you begin is only to quiet your mind and raise your vibration by releasing resistant thoughts.

It's useful not to go into it with the intention of reaching nirvana or receiving Divine guidance or even visualizing your desires. While any of these things can happen, and probably will happen for you at some point, it is as a result of getting to that point of quieting your mind and may even happen after you've finished meditating. After you've finished ten or fifteen minutes of quieting your mind, it is often a great time to ask questions of your Higher Self or to work on a creative project because your connection to Source Energy is heightened.

To begin, however, acknowledge that your intent is only to release resistant thoughts and raise your vibration. Then find something to focus upon such as a word, counting, counting your breaths, or anything that requires a modicum of attention. It took more than a few sessions for me to be able to feel a tingling sensation or numbness, which indicated that I had, at least for brief periods, let go of my constant thoughts.

When I first began meditating I experienced numerous twitches and jerks in my body, which surprised me, but felt like they were an indication that I was releasing resistance. Sometimes my body begins to tingle so much that it is as if there is no feeling in different parts of my body. It is almost as if you can't feel where one body part begins and ends. It is definitely a very natural, pleasurable feeling. There's no sense of losing control. If you don't feel that tingling or numbness or sense of movement in your first few attempts, just let go of any concern about that, knowing you will feel it later. The important thing is to keep allowing yourself that quiet time each day until you find that you can get to that pleasurable detached feeling very easily. Once you've begun to experience that sense of detachment and tingling in your body, you've opened a door to clear communication with your Higher Self, which will release resistance and make you more sensitive to where you're vibrating throughout your day. It's a vital part of learning How to Allow.

Once you've tried meditation for a period of time and are experiencing its benefits, you might want to check into the many books, CD's and guided meditations that are available. I must mention one particular guided meditation by a spiritual practitioner named Meg

Benedicte that involves, among other things, visualizing a spinning vortex around you while you are meditating. It has been explained that our desires, which are being held for us, are maintained in just such a swirling vortex of energy, and that it is our job to get into that vortex. This is what this Allowing business is really all about, getting ourselves into that vortex. So, it makes sense that visualizing the vortex around you can help you to access that energy which creates worlds more easily. See the Recommended Resources Section at the end of this course for more information about the "Unified Field Meditation."

While I have stressed that it is better to enter into meditation with the express purpose of releasing resistance, I alluded earlier to other possibilities that might present themselves as you've become more practiced at meditating. What I often like to do after I've quieted my mind for ten minutes or so and felt the tingling feeling which tells me that I'm truly in a state of meditation, is to ask for guidance from my Higher Self. When I began asking for guidance and receiving clear messages, which often seemed to sound much like my own thoughts, I found it hard to be sure of whether I was really hearing true Divine Guidance. Later, I became aware that the guidance was really being communicated to me in blocks of thought, not exact words, which I was then interpreting. So, it made sense to me that it sounded much like something I would say.

The difference I found was that it was always

reassuring, extremely positive and helpful!! When I was still a little uncertain about the validity of my guidance, I asked for some kind of sign from the Universe that would tell me that I heard my guidance correctly. I would often get the impression of a word, usually a very unusual word which I would then somehow see or hear within a couple of days. For example, recently as I asked for a sign to be on the lookout for, I received the word "ingot." I like the fact that the words I receive are so unusual so that they are something that I wouldn't be expected to see or hear typically. Within a day or two, I was playing a word game on my computer and one of the words I uncovered was, you guessed it, ingot. When I ask for guidance now, I sometimes still ask for that confirmation, conveying to the Universe that I already know that my guidance is real, but that I just enjoy the almost daily surprise of having the word or symbol that was communicated to me appear in the most unlikely way. It helps me to stay on track.

A couple of days ago, I was receiving guidance after meditating, and I received the word and image of a fishhook. What was conveyed with the image was that I was to be teaching people how to fish, as opposed to giving them the fish, a message I'd received before. This meshed perfectly with the internal directive I'd received to complete this course on How to Allow. Although I shouldn't have been surprised, the next day, while out to lunch with friends, I opened the menu and there were several paragraphs describing the fish that were served there along with several drawings of fishhooks. But the confirmation doesn't end there. Two days later, I opened the Sunday newspaper to see a huge photograph covering half of the Business Section containing the images of thirteen large fishhooks illustrating a business article. The Universe constantly amazes me with the way it is able to deliver its message and help you to know that you're being helped and are on your right path.

In addition to possibly asking for guidance at the conclusion of meditation, it is also a good time to visualize something you'd like if it feels good to do so. Sometimes it's much easier to imagine our perfect scenario and focus upon it when we're in that relaxed state. We're also in a resistance-free vibration, which is a match to our desires!

Lesson Five Practice

Because I can't stress enough how important the practice of meditation is to Allowing, I'd like to ask that you make a commitment to yourself to meditate for fifteen minutes each day. It may be one of the most important commitments you make and I've hardly scratched the surface in terms of the benefits you'll receive from this practice. When you've achieved the feeling of quieting your mind for even a brief period and that movement and tingling sensation which will follow, you literally will have opened a door to communication with the non-Physical world which will forever remain open for you. Daily meditation will not only help you to release resistant thoughts but also to be more aware of your emotional guidance, allowing you to shift into better feeling thoughts at earlier stages. It will also enhance your feeling of Well-Being, your confidence that you're not going it alone, and that what you've asked for has already been answered. With that confidence, Allowing follows easily.

Contract

     I,_____, commit, on a daily basis, to quieting my mind for the purpose of releasing my resistant thoughts and tuning up my vibration. This is an important part of my commitment to making feeling good my highest priority. I know that when I honor this commitment, I am aligning with the energy of our Universe and am contributing to creating a higher quality of life for myself and all of the people in my life. My enhanced connection to Source Energy helps me to uplift others as I operate from a place of greater confidence and clarity. I am indeed contributing to the expansion of the consciousness of our world. I know it's worth it!

_____

Lesson Six: Any Blocks? - Releasing False Beliefs

As you have begun incorporating the two Basic Tools into your routine, you should be seeing some things begin to shift in your life. You may not yet have manifested your exact desire, but you may see some evidence that it's on its way to you. What might constitute evidence that your desire is on its way? First, once you understand that Universal forces respond to every one of your desires, you can learn to make your improved mood your evidence that your desires are on their way to you.

That realization can result in an immediate positive shift in your vibration, particularly if you're engaged in asking "Where is it?" or "Why isn't it here yet?" When you begin to trust in the process and know that it works, you can stop yourself in your tracks and say, "I don't need to see any immediate evidence that my reliable new car is on its way to me. The fact that I'm feeling good and trust in the process is my evidence that the car must come. That's the way the laws work."

As you have adjusted your vibration more consistently, however, real concrete evidence that things are shifting does begin to show up. Imagine that you've had problems in your relationship and you are trying to focus on improvement rather than the problematic aspects. After working with the Daily Tune-Up, you notice that your boyfriend, for the first time you can remember, empties the dishwasher without being asked or waiting for you to do it. He also mentions that he really likes the shirt you got him for Christmas, out of the blue. He was so lackluster before, you weren't even sure if he liked it or appreciated it. Maybe he brings you a bouquet of flowers or apologizes for something that happened earlier. None of these events is huge, but they're significant in that they are demonstrating a shifting in the momentum of your relationship.

It's vitally important to notice this sort of evidence and make a point of appreciating it! Write about it in your Daily Tune-up and milk it for all it's worth. Think about it before you go to sleep at night. Focusing on that evidence will attract to you more positive thoughts about your boyfriend until you find yourself focusing more and more on his positive aspects. Before long, mostly positive aspects will be showing up for you in your relationship as you've changed your point of attraction. You simply are no longer a vibrational match to those negative aspects that were causing problems in your relationship.

I've noticed that for many people, however, despite seeing some evidence of positive momentum in some circumstance of their lives, they either pay very little attention to it, continuing to focus on what needs to be fixed, or have a block or "false belief" that prevents them from allowing in their solution.

No matter how much sincere effort you might make to feel good as often as possible, a false belief can prevent you from even imagining a solution to your problem which you could bring to your Daily Tune-up. I'm calling these patterns of thinking false beliefs because I've found it helpful to realize that, in reality, every problem we've created has already been solved and the solution is waiting for us in our vibrational escrow. So any restrictive, limiting belief about why we don't have it or can't have it is, by definition, false. Perhaps, in focusing on reality it seems true on its surface; but, if its solution has already been created by the Universe in response to your desire for improvement, anything that would prevent you from receiving that solution is a false belief.

Before we make an attempt to uncover some of the false beliefs that might be undermining your power to create exactly what you want in your life, I'd like to let a bit of the air out of the concept of beliefs, in general. We've been trained to think that our beliefs are a big deal; we've learned them over a lifetime and they can be impossible to change. Well, that's a belief I don't ascribe to! The spiritual teachers known as Abraham remind us that our beliefs are just thoughts we keep thinking. Nothing more. Doesn't that sound much less ominous?

> *Beliefs, these false limiting beliefs, in particular, are just patterns of thought which can be changed like any other thoughts.*

Let's consider a few possible limiting beliefs that might muddy someone's vibration and interfere with their ability to focus purely on their desire. Imagine a man we'll call Ron who desires lots of money, financial security and the ability to make decisions about what he wants in life without regard to cost. He tells himself that's what he wants but he has an underlying belief that by having more money than he needs he's depriving someone else of the money they need. He sees the financial system as a fixed pie. When one person has an abundance of money, it deprives another person by an equal amount.

Many of us have come to believe now in an ever-expanding universe and understand that one person's financial success doesn't deprive another. In fact, our financial abundance not only allows Source Energy to express more fully through us, but also contributes to the expansion of the financial pie for all of us. As long as Ron has this false belief in scarcity, however, it muddies his vibration when it comes to money and he continues to make just enough money to meet his needs, despite having the wherewithal to attract as much money as he desires.

Some of our false beliefs, however, are less obvious to us and it can take some digging to bring them to our awareness. I'm going to suggest digging, to a limited extent. We don't want to get mired in focusing upon these limiting beliefs or use them as an excuse for why we can't clean up our vibration. Yet, if we can uncover these limiting beliefs and convince ourselves that they are false, we can open up the gate to allowing in the manifestations that have been eluding us.

There is an easy way to unearth these false beliefs, which is much more efficient than traditional psychotherapy, which often has the effect of forcing us to spend years focusing on our problems. And now you know that a continuing focus on our problems will only attract more of the same. A more effective approach for uncovering false beliefs is to return to the list you made in Lesson Two of this course where you wrote down some of your desires. In the Practice for this Lesson, I'll ask you to write down a long list of desires, drawing from that list in Lesson 2. You could add some new desires to your list at this point as you may have already begun to cross some items off your list or may want to re-focus on some new desires.

For each item that you've identified that you want, you'll write below it why you think it hasn't happened yet. When you do this exercise in the space provided below, take your time and let fly the reasons why this desire is not here for you yet. List as many reasons as you can think of.

Bingo, this list of reasons or justifications will identify your limiting beliefs or patterns of thinking that are keeping you from maintaining a pure vibration when it comes to that desire.

I'll offer a couple of examples before asking you to do the exercise. As Part 2 of this exercise, I'd also like to look into some possibilities for releasing the false beliefs you've uncovered with two simple approaches that I've found that have created real shifts for those who've used them. I'd also like to refer you to some powerful techniques developed by others for releasing thought patterns that aren't serving us.

Some of these examples of limiting beliefs have actually come up in going through this process with others:

Desire: To have a happy, fulfilling marriage.

Why I believe it hasn't happened: Most married people aren't happy. My parents divorced and I don't have a role model for a happy marriage. It's impossible to remain happy with someone after years of marriage.

Desire: To have financial success, more money than I need.

Why I believe it hasn't happened: It takes tons of hard work to achieve real financial success. Rich people have a different make-up than the rest of us. Rich people are less spiritual, more selfish. By having more than I need, I'd be depriving someone else.

Desire: To have a healthy, fit body.

Why I believe it hasn't happened: You have to exercise every day to be thin and I don't have time for that. I have a slow metabolism. I don't have the genes to have a healthy body into advanced age. Deterioration of the body is the natural order of things. You can't expect to remain healthy and flexible beyond a certain age.

You can see how, in each case, maintaining any of those beliefs would muddy the vibration you were sending out into the Universe with regard to your desire. It would be like sending a message to the Universe, I want it, but . . .

In an amazing example (for me) of the power of letting go of false beliefs, I cured myself of debilitating back pain a number of years ago. Although I had an intellectual understanding that we create our own reality with our thoughts at that time, I hadn't yet learned how to clean up my vibration in order to Allow my good health. I had developed such horrible back pain that I had resorted to seeing an orthopedic surgeon, had undergone an MRI, and was at times incapacitated by spasms, which would bring me to my knees. The spasms were unpredictable and were seriously interfering with my ability to function.

A fellow parent from one of my sons' soccer teams noticed my obvious pain and suggested a book called *Healing Back Pain—The Mind-Body Connection* by John

Sarno, MD. He mentioned that the book had been discussed on Oprah and that thousands of people had been cured of their back pain after reading this book. I was not only desperate for relief and opposed to surgery, but also extremely receptive to the mind-body connection.

I purchased the book right away and began reading it as I fell asleep that night. I probably had made it about one-third of the way through the book before drifting off to sleep. Up to this point, sleep had been painful, as every time I turned over or shifted position I would feel a sharp pain in my lower back or leg. Sarno stressed the point that back pain had become much like the stomach ulcer of the 1960's, that it was the new acceptable way to manifest the stress in our lives. Doctors had begun using sophisticated x-ray techniques such as MRI's to demonstrate that we had herniated discs or similar physical issues that were causing our pain. Sarno pointed out, however, that there were legions of people walking around with herniated discs, which happened to be discovered during some other procedure, yet these people were experiencing no back pain whatsoever.

That data rang a bell for me when I remembered my orthopedic surgeon telling me that the location of my herniated disc should be causing pain on the opposite side of my back, not the side that was experiencing debilitating spasms. Well, that was enough for me to read. That night, every time I woke up to turn over I reminded myself that "there is nothing wrong with my back." I probably repeated the phrase at least fifty times that night. When I awakened and began walking down the stairs (which usually brought on pain or a spasm), I reminded myself that there was no reason for me to have pain or a spasm from walking down the stairs. There was no pain or spasm. Over the course of that very first day (before I had even finished the book) my back pain began clearing up. By the next day, it was as if I had never had any pain at all.

I had released my belief that there was something physically wrong which needed to be fixed if my back was to be free of pain. Once I received the suggestion that the back pain was merely a manifestation of stress, and that there was nothing physically wrong with me, I began to operate as if there was nothing wrong; my symptoms vanished. It is amazing how powerful the release of erroneous thoughts can be in helping us to reconnect with our natural alignment with Well-Being. Be mindful of that as you do the following exercise, which is designed to help you to uncover any false beliefs that may be hindering you from achieving the things you desire. Really take the time to explore any unexamined thoughts that might be serving to bring down your vibration.

Lesson Six Practice (Part A)

Make a long list of your desires, even those that aren't at the top of your mind at the moment. Making this list is largely for the purpose of uncovering some beliefs that might be hampering your ability to make progress toward any of your goals. For each item, below it list the reasons you think it hasn't materialized for you. There you'll find your false beliefs.

Desire or Intention:

_____
_____
_____
_____
_____
_____

Why I think it hasn't happened yet:

_____
_____
_____
_____
_____
_____
_____

Lesson Six Practice (Part B)

Once you've surprised yourself by coming up with some false beliefs that may be clouding your vibration when it comes to your desires, you need to think about what might work for you in letting go of those inhibiting thoughts. You may simply be able to point out to yourself how ridiculous they are, how they were formed during a time when you knew so much less than you do now, and just let them die a natural death.

If any limiting beliefs you uncovered seem to keep cropping up, however, there are many materials out there that deal with releasing false beliefs. I won't attempt here to go into great detail as to how each might best work, as I've found that the effectiveness of the tools really vary by individual. After all, we developed these beliefs from our own life experiences and what it will take for us to release or refute them is necessarily unique to each of us.

I have found, however, what seems to be one of the most common reasons given by most people for not achieving their desires as well as a method that has worked well for releasing this particular block. For nearly everyone there seems to be someone out there who they believe has prevented them from being a healthy thriving adult who can have whatever they desire. There is someone who has done something to them, which they just can't forgive, and their blame continues to block them from having a positive vibration.

I have found that in these cases forgiveness, in general, is often a necessary means of Allowing in their Well-Being. Because the need for forgiveness seems to crop up for nearly everyone I talk with, I'd like to take a moment to suggest a way of thinking about forgiveness, which has worked well for me, and some of the clients and friends I've suggested it to.

Before I suggest one approach to the topic of forgiveness, let's get ourselves into a more powerful state of mind so that we are really in a position to let go of any blame we're holding onto. Now that you understand how the Law of Attraction works and that no one else can create in your experience but you, it's easier to let quite a few more people off the hook, isn't it? What someone has done may seem unforgivable, but you attracted that person and that aspect of him or her into your experience by virtue of your own vibration. In other words, there are no victims. And, despite how angry you might feel about how someone has treated you, it feels much better to feel angry than to feel like a victim.

Viewing the situation in this way takes much of the power away from the person who has wronged you and helps you to reclaim your own power. Once you've acknowledged that you weren't a victim and feel your power coming back, it becomes easier to release the anger, even very justified anger, toward that person.

Almost everyone has some situation they could point to where the behavior of someone was so destructive that it seems to be really unforgivable. It could be dysfunctional or abusive parents, a former spouse who wronged you or the boss who fired you without justification. While nearly everyone has someone to point to who has had such a negative impact on their life at some point that they consider them unforgivable, I'd like to suggest that finding a way to forgive them is one of the best things you could do for yourself.

I want to stress that this forgiveness is for you, not for them. You've probably heard that by holding onto the blame you have for this unforgivable person, you're allowing them to live on in your head rent-free. They've moved on, could probably care less and are going on with their life, and yet you're continuing to allow your thoughts about them to deny you the Well-Being you deserve. In forgiving them, you would not be condoning their despicable actions or acknowledging that anything they did was okay. You'd be forgiving them because you no longer want to carry the burden of thinking about them and what they did. You no longer want to blame yourself for letting them do what they did. You want to move on and focus on the things you could be creating in your life which have nothing to do with them.

One of the most powerful statements regarding forgiveness, which has helped me to forgive when I didn't think I could, was made by Dr. Wayne Dyer in his book *The Power of Intention*. He suggested that when we look at the person's rotten behavior, we recognize that the person who acted that way was doing the best that they could at the time or they would've done better. Now stop yourself for a second before you think, "Oh they could've done lots better." When you really think about it, by definition, if the person could have done better, they would have. That's all they had in them at the time.

When you think of any situation that way, it becomes much easier to practice forgiveness. I've used this way of thinking time and time again to forgive people for real and probably imagined slights and even things which seemed unforgivable to me at the time. They were doing the best they could do, period. End of discussion. It doesn't matter that they should've known better or how reprehensible their conduct was, that was all they had. And, if that was all they had, why would I continue to waste my time blaming them for not having the ability to do better? This way of thinking works for me, often. And I've found that the inability to forgive someone is often at the heart of our failure to clean up our vibration on a number of subjects. The vibration of blame or feeling that something has gone wrong here which can never be fixed, doesn't allow us to make peace with where we are, the essential foundation of Allowing our Well-Being.

So, for this practice, think about anyone you think you might still need to forgive, as a means of helping yourself to feel even better. Make a list of any people who have wronged you. Again, we won't focus on this for long so as not to activate the unwanted vibration associated with your bad experience. Go through the list. You might even be able to make it humorous, depending upon how petty or truly malicious someone's actions were. In each case, think about how that person really was doing the best they could do at that time. Remember that, by definition, if they could've done better, they would have! See if you can generate some forgiveness and notice if you feel less resistance after the process.

People I Could Forgive:

Another methodology which I uncovered in teaching myself How to Allow is something known as The Sedona Method. This isn't necessarily a means to refute false beliefs, although it can operate that way; it is more a way of releasing unwanted thoughts when talking yourself into a better view of the situation just isn't working. Sometimes, no matter how much effort you make to work with an unwanted thought and work yourself into better ways of thinking about the situation, you feel like you just can't let go of it. The Sedona Method is based on the work of Lester Levenson, a man who cured himself of several life-threatening illnesses over a period of three months by using a tool he developed for letting go of limiting thoughts.

In a nutshell, The Sedona Method is based on two key principles: (1) thoughts and feelings are not facts and they are not the real you; and (2) you are capable of letting those thoughts and feelings go. The letting go process is so simple that I couldn't imagine it would actually work when I first learned it. It involves focusing on an issue you'd like to feel better about and letting yourself really experience the feeling it brings up for you. You then ask yourself if you *could* let this particular feeling go? Your answer could be yes or no, although you are working toward being able to let it go. You then ask yourself if you *would* let this feeling go? If the answer is no or maybe, you would ask yourself whether you would rather have this feeling or be free? Even if the answer is still no, you would ask the simple question, "*When would I let this feeling go?*" At this point, you might think *now* and be able to just let it go or you might need to repeat the process a few times until you feel like you are free of that particular feeling. I have hardly done justice to the Sedona Method and am really summarizing it to give you a general idea of it's simplicity and effectiveness.

I would wholeheartedly recommend reading and digesting *The Sedona Method, Your Key to Lasting Happiness, Success, Peace and Emotional Well-being,* by Hale Dwoskin. They also offer courses on the Sedona Method. Please see additional references in the Recommended Resources at the end of this course. This method is a handy tool to have in your bag of tricks when you just can't seem to let go of a recurring false belief that is clouding your pure vibration and interfering with the Allowing of your Well-Being.

Another method I came across for releasing false beliefs has become known as "The Work," by Byron Katie. Katie had a transformative experience during her own dark night of the soul, realizing that all human suffering comes from believing our thoughts. Her epiphany led her to develop this process of asking four simple questions about any limiting beliefs:

1. Is it true?

2. Can you absolutely know that it's true?

3. How do your respond when you believe that thought?

4. Who would you be without that thought?

Katie then asks that you apply something she calls a "turnaround statement," a statement expressing the opposite of your thought or belief. The turnaround is a way to attempt to experience the truth of the opposite of what you believe. Many people have had great success with this technique and, in giving you only the general thrust of "The Work," I have not begun to do it justice. Please see the Recommended Resources at the end of this course for additional information regarding "The Work."

My intent in this section is not to add on a multitude of tools and exercises that you might feel you need to complete in order to Allow the Well-Being that is natural to you.

My intent is rather to provide a crystal clear understanding of how subtle shifts in your thinking and hence, your vibration, operate to attract both what you want and what you don't want into your life. My goal is to simplify the whole Allowing process by providing a daily ritual consisting of two powerful tools which will take you most of the way toward Allowing all of your desires into your experience.

I want to reiterate that having too many tools which we think we need to be applying, on an inconsistent basis, can lead us to feel like we're not doing enough and aren't doing a good job at maintaining our vibration. There is no need to make it hard!

Nonetheless, in my experience, I've seen that many people, including me, needed to let go of some underlying erroneous beliefs that were hampering their ability to create their perfect script during their Daily Tune-Up. With that caveat, if you do find yourself needing to challenge a false belief, or can't seem to let go of a counterproductive thought, I'd recommend exploring your ability to forgive, checking out "The Work" or learning The Sedona Method, all of which are powerful means of letting go of negative thoughts which may be interfering with your vibration.

Lesson Seven: Allowing Improved Relationships

While this program is dedicated to providing simple practical rituals which can be used consistently to Allow your own natural Well-Being, I have rarely encountered a friend, loved one, or client that didn't perceive one of their biggest obstacles to happiness to be an important relationship in their life. And, while it's *your* vibration we're talking about here, to the extent that you believe someone else's behavior is affecting your vibration, you're not honoring your commitment to making feeling good your highest priority. I know, I know, when someone in your life is *"making you feel miserable,"* it's not that easy to maintain your pure positive vibration and to expect better things from them. Yet, this is exactly where your focus needs to be if you are to maintain your connection to your Source and create wonderful things in your life.

It is said that you cannot create in the reality of another, nor can they create in yours. It's an inside job and we each are the creators of our own realities. It becomes confusing, though, and sometimes maddening, when you are naturally involved with other people, whether at work, in your family, or in your friendships, and it feels as if the things they are doing are causing you to have experiences you'd rather not have. The most helpful thing to remember in situations where a relationship is the source of contrast in your life is that you are in charge of your vibration. In fact, when you find yourself stewing about another's behavior, the fact that you, not them, are in charge of your vibration, can be a helpful mantra to repeat to yourself to remove your focus from their behavior.

While we each are responsible for creating our own experiences, if you have someone else's aspects in your experience that you don't like, you've brought them there by your continuing attention to them. Isn't that a revolutionary thought? There are no victims here. You may not have initiated that person's negative behaviors that keep showing up for you but, by your habit of thought about them, you've achieved vibrational harmony with those negative aspects and keep summoning them. When you are able to remove your focus from the aspects of the person that are bothersome to you, and instead focus on their positive aspects, the negative aspects will stop showing up for you. You simply won't be a vibrational match to them any longer and they can't come into your experience.

It probably wasn't your fault to begin with. Perhaps that person began demonstrating aspects of themselves that you didn't like as time went on; they literally trained you into expecting that kind of offering from them. In many relationships, there is simply a habit of thought or expectation that developed over time and these patterns of behavior continue because they are a match to your vibration.

So, to improve any relationship, the best thing that you can do is to think of every positive aspect of that person that you can and make an effort to focus on them as often as possible. The less desirable aspects will begin to show up less and less as you're no longer attracting them; in turn, it will become easier to focus on the positive aspects because there will be more of them to focus upon.

This can be difficult in a long-standing relationship where strong habits of thought have been formed. In cases like that, it is often easier to focus on earlier days in the relationship when the person was demonstrating all of their best qualities. When you do your Daily Tune-Up, make it a point to write about their strengths, the nice things they've done for you, even if some of these things need to be remembered from an earlier time. You'll be amazed at how quickly this positive focus can begin to improve a relationship, as the person will be responding vibrationally to your new focus almost immediately.

Several years ago a good friend who knew nothing about the Law of Attraction was sharing with me some issues she'd had with her husband, which would be hard for anyone to recover from. Her husband, while charming at times, had exhibited some pretty bad behavior, untrustworthiness and a real lack of compassion for his wife. I have to admit that I was shocked to learn that they were now getting along much better and were taking a trip to Europe together. I was surprised to see what appeared to be a genuine turnaround in the relationship and asked her what had happened to bring about the change? She responded that, after forgiving her husband for his transgressions, which took some time, she just started to ignore the things that he did which frustrated her and those behaviors just began to disappear. Instead he was returning to the person he had been when they first married. She said, "We just have so much fun together." I shouldn't have been surprised when I learned about her change of focus but those were dramatic results, to say the least.

I know it can seem impossible to think of the positive aspects of someone when it feels like it would be so much more satisfying to stew over their rotten behavior. You feel angry and you're completely justified. When you realize that by continuing to focus on their rotten behavior you're only attracting more of the same, however, it's an excellent motivator to move on from your anger as quickly as you can. The side benefit is that you will immediately begin to feel so much better as you think of the person as you'd like them to be rather than how they're behaving at the moment. The whole quality of your day will improve as you begin to attract similarly vibrating positive thoughts that generate more momentum.

You can literally create a fantasy about someone who is in your life and they will begin to modify their behavior to meet your fantasy, because you simply will not be attracting the undesirable parts of them into your experience. Those less desirable aspects of their personality might show up for others, but you will no longer be attracting them.

If someone with whom you have a relationship has so many undesirable aspects and can't demonstrate enough of the positive aspects that you're attracting through your new higher vibration, they may simply move out of your experience easily and naturally because there is no longer a vibrational match between you.

By focusing on a person's most positive aspects, you're not manipulating them in any way, as we all have creative control over our behavior and experiences. You are merely evoking the most positive parts of them that were always there; they just weren't evident when you were mostly focusing on the negative behaviors that were getting your attention.

So, by focusing on a person's positive aspects, you're actually helping them to be their best self. You're using your connection to your Source to be a powerful influence that their Inner Being is responding to, which is bringing out the best in them. This can be true whether you're thinking your best thoughts about your children, your spouse, a co-worker or neighbor. You'll be amazed at the changes you'll witness in other people's behavior when you train yourself to expect the best from them.

A client I'll call Linda told me a funny story about her recent vacation with her family. Her husband, for reasons unbeknownst to her, had become moody and withdrawn and was casting a pall over their family time by the pool. Linda was disappointed, her first thoughts being, "Why would he act like this now? Here we are on our family vacation in a wonderful place. We could be having so much fun and instead I'm feeling on edge, like he's having no fun and the day is ruined."

She quickly remembered her commitment to making feeling good her highest priority and decided to ignore his moodiness. She spent a few moments lying back on her beach chair, imagining him smiling, engaging her in conversation and telling her about the book he was reading, suggesting that she might enjoy it. An hour or so later, when she had returned to their hotel room, her husband walked up to her with a smile, not a trace of moodiness and said, "I really think you'd enjoy this book. You ought to read it too." It seems amazing but we are all really a powerful influence in the lives of others when we choose to focus on the way we want things to be rather than our present reality.

I have been especially elated over the powerful influence we can have over our own children when we hold the highest possible vision for them. As parents, we've been trained that worry is a normal state when it comes to our children and that we need to be on constant alert to protect them. Knowing what I now know about the way the Universe works, I'm very careful to nip any worries in the bud when they arise. I remind myself that my children are amazing, intelligent, capable people and that they have their own emotional guidance system, which is leading them toward thoughts and activities that feel better.

If something is going on in one of their lives, which I could choose to worry about, I make it a point to shift as quickly as possible to reminding myself of how capable they are and I envision them happy and having great success at whatever they are involved in at the time. I wouldn't want to violate the privacy of any of them by relating stories of their successes in these situations (because they'd be really annoyed), but I can tell you that I know from experience that you can be a powerful influence for your kids by holding your highest thoughts about them. Their Well-Being is natural and your positive focus is a beacon, which helps them to be called forward toward that vortex of Well-Being.

> *Remember that your greatest advantage to others is seeing in them what they would like to see in themselves.*

One aspect of relationships that can be confusing as we are learning to become deliberate creators, are occasions in which we are co-creating with another, such as in a work or family situation. We may be working together toward a common goal, but feel that the other person is at odds with us over some aspect of our creation. Perhaps one of you wants to renovate your home while the other is opposed to the idea because of the cost involved. You might be dreaming of purchasing a vacation home and one of you would prefer that it be in the mountains while the other would only be happy near the beach. This seeming contradiction can lead to a sense of frustration or futility as you may feel like it's impossible to create a situation that will please you both.

In cases like this, it's best to ignore the details when you focus on your desire. After all, what you really want, the essence of your desire is harmony and a beautiful home where you will enjoy each other's company. Maintain your focus on the harmony, the beautiful home, leaving out the details of the renovation or location if it causes any negative emotion when you think about it. Allow the Universe to come up with a clever and much better solution than you could dream up, which will give everyone involved the essence of his or her desire.

> *When even one party is aligned with Source Energy in the co-creative process, I've seen amazing instances of pieces falling into place to give everyone what they wanted when it seemed impossible.*

Lesson Seven Practice

Make a list of the important people in your life and write down as many positive aspects of them as you can think of. Refer to this often and add to it as they've shown you more of their best self. Refer to this list when you feel challenged by some circumstances that are causing disharmony in your relationship. If something in any of your relationships is troubling you before you begin your Daily Tune-Up, refer back to your list of that person's positive aspects as a way to get yourself in the right frame of mind for making peace with where you are and writing about your desires as if they've already manifested for you.

Lesson Eight: Helpful Tips for Staying on Track

Once I began doing the daily rituals, I found it much easier to notice any negative emotion I was experiencing and to make a correction in my thinking. The two daily rituals, by putting you into a state of positive vibration more consistently, raise your vibrational set point, the vibration you gravitate toward naturally. They literally begin to change the pathways in your brain so that it becomes easier and easier to choose better feeling thoughts. And, as you're choosing better feeling thoughts more often, you're becoming a magnet to other higher vibrating thoughts.

That being said, of course, situations will continue to present themselves that cause you to react with negative thoughts and the accompanying negative emotion. Luckily, as you raise your vibration, these occurrences become less frequent, but life will continue to present new situations that will cause you to desire improvement. That's the way we experience our expansion in this physical experience. So, it's good to have some tricks in your arsenal that will help you to make the shift to better feeling thoughts when you find yourself experiencing that negative emotion which is your communication from your emotional guidance system that you're out of alignment.

It is really helpful to think of negative emotion as perfect feedback from your emotional guidance system, letting you know that the way you are thinking about your situation differs from the way your Source or Inner Being would view it. Right away, that attitude takes a bit of the wind out of your negative emotion. When you can actually appreciate the negative emotion, even a little, as much needed feedback that you're out of alignment, you're already on your way to relief. A better feeling is now much closer. And, if you can manage to appreciate your awareness of your negative emotion, you've avoided the possibility of creating additional negative thoughts by faulting yourself for having the negative emotion in the first place.

So, one of the first tricks to keep in your arsenal is to pat yourself on the back for your newfound awareness of your negative emotion. Your first response to finding yourself feeling frustration, sadness or anger can be, "I'm glad I'm recognizing that I'm having this negative emotion. I'm becoming more sensitive to my negative emotion and now I have the chance to shift my thinking to something that is going to feel better and create better results in my life."

One trick I've found which can be helpful to use when there is a subject which you keep gravitating toward which causes you to experience negative emotion, is to make a decision that you've turned that subject over to the Universe and are getting out of the way. The subject needs no more attention. Because the Universe is on it, you need only to change your focus to what you want instead. Once you've made that pronouncement to yourself, whenever the subject pops into your head say, "Oh yeah, I almost forgot, I've already decided what I want for that one; I don't have to think about it."

Imagine, for example, that you're worrying about the state of your bank balance. Continuing to focus on the amount of the balance and your bills will only serve to perpetuate the feeling and the reality of lack. As the subject comes up, try to say to yourself, "I've done the best I can and I've turned it over to the Universe. I'm choosing instead to think about how good it feels to have an overflowing bank account and all of the money I need to pay my bills." Later, thoughts of your bank balance come up again and you say to yourself, "Oh yeah, I almost forgot, I've already decided I'm having a huge balance in my bank account. Source is on it; I don't need to think about that right now." This dialogue can help you to let go of nagging worries, in particular. I generally feel better just knowing that I've stopped the negative thinking and that I've spent a few moments focusing on the outcome that I want. When I do that, I know things will get better. That's the way the laws work!

One other helpful way of thinking regarding the enormous power of your positive vibration, which I've alluded to, is that the power of a high vibration is exponentially more powerful than a low level negative vibration. That explains why things can often be turned around fairly easily. It doesn't take an equal number of minutes of positive vibration to cancel out your minutes of negatively obsessing about something. That knowledge can often help you to improve your vibration immediately!

What is almost amazing and great to know, is that a thought reaches a point where it gathers some creative power after only 17 seconds of pure undiluted focus. That's right, only 17 seconds! After 17 seconds it draws another thought to it and becomes exponentially more powerful. After 34 seconds of pure focus, the next thought combusts and ratchets up to an even higher level of energy. Once you've continued a pure strain of thought for 68 seconds (just 4 of those 17 second segments), you've added enough force to it that the object of your focus is on its way to manifestation. You need only make an effort to focus as often as you can on the positive side of your desires rather than the things you're hoping to change.

Seventeen seconds is a very small segment of time, yet most of us contradict our pure positive thought even within that 17-second segment. Imagine yourself thinking, I really want to get that job *but there are so many other qualified people trying for it.* Or, I'd really like to take that vacation this summer, *but it's too expensive for me right now.* So, it's really important to be aware of how you're thinking and to make that 17, 34 or 68 seconds of thought pure, positive and undiluted!

The spiritual teachers known as Abraham have offered that 17 seconds of pure positive thought is worth about 2000 hours of action taken. 34 seconds is worth 20,000 hours. And, 68 seconds is worth about 2,000,000 hours of effort! If you can really get a handle on the power of your positive focus and believe in it, there is no way you would not find the time to stop for 68 seconds several times a day to visualize a positive outcome to a situation in your life which you'd like to change. Think of this as leveraging your energy.

I've seen that by doing the daily rituals over a fairly short period of time, you actually strengthen your ability to focus, that is, to hold your attention positively upon the object of your desire without muddying your vibration with contrary thoughts. Before I began using the Daily Tune-Up and meditating each day, I found it hard to just sit down and visualize what I wanted, even for 68 seconds. My mind would wander and I'd invariably find myself creeping back toward the negative subject I was trying to change. Because meditation makes you more sensitive to negative emotion and because the daily writing process trains you to visualize your desired outcome, it does become easier to stop throughout your day and focus on exactly what you do want. And, that can make all the difference in your ability both to feel good and to attract all of the things that you desire.

So, once you've gotten into the habit of using the daily rituals, I'd definitely recommend stopping for 68 seconds or more several times a day to focus on your desires. Try to focus on them for the purpose of feeling good, if you can, rather than for attaining your desires. That way, your vibration is more pure and not clouded with the fact that you don't already have what you want. Begin with little issues, which you don't care about as much, and as you attract those things you'll build confidence both in your own ability to focus and the reliability of the Universe. Then it will just keep getting better and better and better!

Another helpful tool for staying on track as you're learning to manifest the things you want and things are still changing, is to remind yourself that your mood is your evidence of the physical manifestation of your desires. Once you've seen some evidence of success, and you trust the process, you need to relish your knowledge that the laws work, and that you therefore **know** that when you make your mood your top priority, the things you want are coming into your experience.

> *If you can make the best of whatever you're focused upon, then you can rely on the fact that your future will be better than what is.*

As things are changing, there invariably will be times when life throws you a curve ball and you find it impossible to choose better thoughts about the subject. Perhaps you've just received some terrible news about a loved one, received a financial blow, or had a fight with your significant other, which has left you beside yourself with anger. In those cases, it's often best to use distraction to get yourself out of the negative spiral.

You know that you're only attracting more undesired "stuff" into your life if you remain mired in such negative emotion, but sometimes it's just ridiculously difficult to try to choose better feeling thoughts. That can be the time to watch a movie, take a nap, do something you enjoy, take your dog for a walk, meditate, anything you can do to distract yourself until you can allow yourself to feel a little bit better about the situation. When you're facing a situation that is just too hard to think your way out of in the moment, pat yourself on the back for taking any action you can to remove your focus from it until you can get your bearings again.

Another tool for staying on track when you think things aren't moving quickly enough and you're wondering if you're even a good creator, is to focus on the fact that what you're trying to create is so specific and wonderful that the Universe isn't delivering it to you until it's got all of the aspects you want. After all, do you want to attract the just "okay" relationship that is a vibrational match to you as you are right now, or the soul mate relationship that is being lined up for you as your vibration continues to rise? Do you want to get the first job that comes along or the job that meets all of your needs? Imagine the Universe creating and lining up the perfect circumstances for you as you focus on your desire. Allow the Universe to figure out the "how's" of bringing in your desire while you give it your pure, undiluted focus.

One issue that often comes up for people trying to manifest a desire that seems far from where they find themselves, is that they aren't sure how it could come about. They aren't even sure of the details of what they want because it's hard to imagine how it would fit in with their current reality. Because the Universe has heard every one of your requests and knows what you really, really want, often it is in a better place to choose how your desire will manifest and to fill in the details. This is the time to focus on your end result and leave the "how's" and the details up to the Universe. By focusing on your end result, or the essence of your desire, you're giving the Universe wide latitude to come up with something even better than you might have imagined.

What I'm suggesting here is that you get excited about your end result and even have fun writing about or imagining the details of receiving your desire, but that you remain unattached to the details of how your desire will play out, how it will come to you. Think of the details in a light way, as if it doesn't really matter if your wish comes to you in that particular way. It's just fun to think about it that way. You've put out your request for the essence of your desire and the Universe is now working backwards to fill in the details, the people, places, events and circumstances that will allow your desire to come to you in all of it's glory.

On the other hand, if you can imagine your desire in magnificent detail while being free of any resistance, generating only pure positive emotion when you think about it, absolutely go with that!

> *Being free of resistance when you focus on your desire is the key. Being vague and resistance free is better than being specific with resistance. Being specific in your focus with no resistance is best of all because it generates the pure positive emotion and excitement, which really lines you up with your desire!*

Lesson Eight Practice

Always making the Daily Tools and feeling good as often as possible your top priority, stop several times a day and focus on a desire for 68 seconds or more of pure undiluted thought. Make a note of any changes you see in the coming days and weeks in response to your new focus.

Lesson Nine: Inspired Action—Living Life in the Field of Appreciation

As I continue to learn How to Allow, I've seen that my actions are becoming more and more about timing and inspiration than effort. I no longer dive into tasks or activities if I'm not feeling lined up with what I'm trying to accomplish. Remember how many hours of action are equivalent to 68 seconds of positive focus? It's always worth taking a moment to try to line up your energy on any subject before taking action.

In an example of cleaning up your vibration before acting, I recently was able to turn around what appeared to be an obstacle into a great demonstration of the unwavering support of the Universe. I had overlooked making an important hotel reservation for a college family weekend and our whole family was really looking forward to it. There was no way we could miss it! There were at least 30 hotels in the city, but once outside the city, nothing remotely close to the school. Apparently, hotel rooms were booked as much as a year in advance and, with the big weekend only one month away, I felt panicked about finding room at the inn! I made calls to several hotels while in that mental state of worry and, as expected, they had all been booked solid for months. I did get a few laughs from the reservation clerks, though. None of them even offered wait lists.

I realized that I would need to change my vibration on this issue if I was to have any chance of success.

Every time I thought of family weekend and our lack of accommodations, I got a sinking feeling in my stomach. Then I reprimanded myself for not making reservations months ago because I had been warned about the demand for hotel space. I knew that it would be futile to continue to call hotels with that mindset. So . . . I waited, and waited, until the date got closer and closer, and kept working on my expectations about the hotel room. I knew that my waiting was, on the surface, contrary to what most people would think I should have been doing, which was calling every hotel in the city and pleading for a room. Instead, I kept waiting and began to think about all of the good things that happen for me when my energy is lined up. I also focused on how much fun we would have as a family that weekend, leaving out any focus on where we would stay. I pictured us happy, laughing, having a good time together, period.

As we were closing in on the weekend, now about a week away, my son called and asked how I was doing with finding a hotel? He mentioned that his friends in similar circumstances had found that there were no vacancies within ninety minutes of the University. My first thought was, "Yikes," but then I had a better thought. At that moment, I had just been having a great conversation with my son, was feeling good, and was thinking about how fun it would be to spend the weekend with him. I was really excited about seeing him and meeting his friends. I told him, as confidently as I could, that I hadn't found anything yet but that I knew we'd work something out. I really reached for confidence at that moment, because I realized that I was not only trying to buck up my own expectations, but I was also telling my son that I knew things would work out.

As I hung up the phone, I knew then that now was my time to act. I immediately called one of the nearby hotels I had tried previously. They responded, without hesitation, that they had one room available, and that it was the last room in the hotel. I was floored, and of course, incredibly grateful. I should not have been so surprised, as it was a great reminder to me of the importance of lining up my energy before taking any action and of maintaining my positive expectation and faith in the helpfulness of the Universe!

When we begin to operate more often in our vibrational vortex where all of our solutions lie, decisions can also become less monumental. We can approach our decisions by imagining either option and how each possible scenario makes us feel. We should obviously go with the decision that gives us the better feeling when we imagine it; that decision is more in alignment with our true intent.

That being said, once a decision has been made, knowing what you now know about lining up your energy, there really is only one thing to do. Upon making your decision, line up with that course of action. Don't second guess yourself or spend time imagining a better outcome if you had opted for the other choice. Thinking about the other option will only muddy your vibration with respect to the decision you've made. This is an opportunity to create the best scenario you can by focusing on all of the positive aspects of your decision and going with it. You'll find it's often less important which decision you make than that you line up your energy in a positive way with the option you've chosen.

As we're spending more time in the vicinity of our vibrational reality, where all of our desires are gathered, we begin to notice more and more synchronicities, those surprising occurrences that just can't be random and reflect a greater force at work behind the scenes. These synchronicities, or communications from the Universe, can help us to feel that we're on track, that our efforts at alignment are bringing us closer to Who We Really Are and our desires.

These out of the blue occurrences always boost my morale and reinforce my feeling of being connected to Source Energy. In a wonderful example, I was once in New York City with my family for the Thanksgiving holiday, where the weather was fairly chilly, and a pretty remarkable sign appeared. I had always had an affinity for butterflies and often they would fly up to me, sometimes landing on my chair and even on my shoulder. In the summer, hardly a day would go by when a butterfly didn't cross my path. I always took that as a sign from the Universe that I was being supported. On this particular weekend, however, November in New York City, it was far too cold for butterflies and we were also staying on a very high floor of a high-rise hotel. I looked out the window as we were about to head out and couldn't believe it when I saw a bright orange butterfly (a real one, not a float!) flying outside our window on the twelfth floor. Not only was it too cold for butterflies, but we were extremely high up for any butterfly to reach, and this butterfly looked like none I had ever seen before. I had to show the rest of my family so they would believe it wasn't my imagination. It was absolutely stunning and quite a message from the Universe.

On another occasion, I was flying coast to coast and thought it would be really nice to fly first class. I had no desire, though, to pay the first class fare, which was far out of proportion to the coach fare. For a couple of weeks before my flight, each time I thought about it, I thought to myself that I would take a first class seat if it were only fifty dollars extra. I actually had no idea what the cost of a first class upgrade would be or of its availability, but fifty dollars seemed like the amount I'd be willing to spend for the experience of flying first class on such a long flight. When I arrived at the ticket counter to check my luggage, I asked if there were any upgrades available. I later learned that there are hardly ever any upgrades available as business travelers usually pre-reserve those seats with their frequent flier miles. But, surprisingly, the agent said they had one seat available for fifty dollars. I was delighted and really enjoyed the larger seat, the delicious meal and wine. It was a great flight. On my return, I mentioned to the ticket agent on the opposite coast that I had gotten the first class upgrade on the way out and she said that a mistake must have been made. There were no upgrades for fifty dollars; they were one hundred fifty dollars, at a minimum. She couldn't understand how it could have happened. In this case, my lack of knowledge about the true cost of the upgrade caused me to have just the right expectation that would allow my desire to make its way to me.

These kinds of things happen often for me when I've made an effort to line up my energy. The great thing is that the more often you line up with your vibrational reality and get used to that sensation, the easier and more natural it becomes. You actually train yourself to those better feeling vibrations. And, that's what this journey and this course is all about.

As you've made your way through this course, from committing to making feeling good your highest priority, to making peace with where you are right now, and to the daily rituals of tuning up your vibration and meditation, you may have noticed that a common thread of this program is moving yourself into the field of *Appreciation*.

> *Appreciation is defined as the recognition of the quality, value, significance or magnitude of people and things.*

The spiritual teachers known as Abraham have said that an appreciation of yourself and others are the closest vibrational matches to God or Source Energy of anything witnessed in this Universe.

As you have begun to master the process of Allowing your full connection with Source Energy and achieved some success in creating the circumstances you want in your life, you have undoubtedly developed a greater appreciation for yourself and others and for our joint willingness to do our best to become more deliberate creators in this physical existence.

What is also likely to develop as you Allow in more of your Well-Being, is a profound appreciation for the fact that Source Energy answers every one of your requests. This is no small thing. It is truly amazing, when you think of it! Every single time we express a desire for something, a cast of thousands goes straight to work to fulfill that desire in the best way possible for us. It is almost impossible not to feel incredible gratitude and appreciation. It is this appreciation for the ways the laws of the Universe work, and the incredible resources working on your behalf, which *Allows* you to have faith in your fondest desires before you've seen any evidence of them in your life.

This state of mind, this faith in what is at work here, draws us into our vortex, into the field of Appreciation, a state of being in alignment with Who We Really Are, an extension of Source Energy having a physical experience on this earth plane. And, by learning how to align our energy to create on this earth plain, we are naturally drawn to living on our Soul's path, to living our life's purpose.

In living a more Soul-driven life, as we make happiness our highest priority, we naturally turn outward and realize our profound connection with others. By making happiness our highest goal, we naturally uplift all of those around us upon whom we are focused. Life begins to take on a new meaning when we realize our true nature as powerful creators.

As we've entered this field of Appreciation, for ourselves and others, and for the Infinite Intelligence of the Universe, life is bound to get better and better and better. As more and more things you want come easily into your experience, people will begin to ask, "What's happened to you? You seem to be happy most of the time. Things seem to come so easily for you. You just seem to magically get things you want to go your way." And you do.

A Final Reminder of Your Work for this Course:

1. *Commit to making feeling as good as you can your highest priority. You won't just try, but <u>will</u> choose the best thoughts you can whenever you can.*

2. *Make peace with where you are. Remember that nothing has gone wrong here and you can get anywhere from here. Find things to appreciate in your current situation. Incredible manifestations often occur from this shift alone!*

3. *Practice the Daily Tune up writing process every day.*

4. *Meditate every day.*

5. *Know then that you've done your work and that anything else you might do is extra. Expect continued improvement. When you think of it, spend some 68 second or more intervals each day thinking about what you want and why you want it.*

Remember that there are no limits here except for your own imagination. I can't wait to hear about what you create and the joy you'll experience as you master *How to Allow*! Please contact me at *Susan@howtoallow.net* to share your successes. I'd love to hear from you.

Recommended Resources

There are many amazing books and other materials on the Law of Attraction and deliberate creation and this list doesn't begin to scratch the surface. In my effort to keep it simple, I've just included those that were referred to in this course.

Meg Benedicte can be contacted at http://www.soulfulservices.com. Her Unified Field Meditation CD is available there.

Braden, Gregg. *Secrets of the Lost Mode of Prayer: The Hidden Power of Beauty, Blessings, Wisdom and Hurt.* Carlsbad: Hay House, Inc., 2006.

Dooley, Mike. *Infinite Possibilities, The Art of Living Your Dreams.* New York: Atria Books, 2009.

Dwoskin, Hale. *The Sedona Method, Your Key To Lasting Happiness, Success, Peace and Emotional Well-Being.* Sedona: Sedona Press, 2003.

Dyer, Dr. Wayne. *The Power of Intention, Learning to Co-create Your World Your Way.* Carlsbad: Hay House, Inc., 2005.

Hicks, Jerry and Esther. *Ask and It is Given, Learning to Manifest Your Desires.* Carlsbad: Hay House, Inc., 2004.

http://www.abraham-hicks.com

Katie, Byron. *Loving What Is: Four Questions That Can Change Your Life.* New York: Harmony Books, 2002.

http://www.thework.com.

Maw, Jeannette. *The Magic of Pray Rain Journaling.* http://www.goodvibecoach.com

Walsch, Neal Donald. *Conversations with God: Book 1: An Uncommon Dialogue.* New York: G.P. Putnam's Sons, 1996.

www.HowToAllow.net
© 2017 Susan Shearer Young

In addition to posting her blog, "The Art of Allowing," on all subjects related to the Law of Attraction from her site, www.howtoallow.net, Susan Shearer Young is a Life Coach and founder of *"Inside Job Life Coaching—Shifting Your Inner Game and Creating Life Changes Through Inspired Action."*

Susan's clients have made major shifts in their vibrations and had life-changing results in every area of their lives, including finances, relationships, feelings of self-worth, career and, most importantly, their level of happiness.

WHAT CLIENTS HAVE TO SAY ABOUT COACHING WITH SUSAN SHEARER YOUNG

I can't wait to tell u howwwwww amazing last week's tools worked. 180 degree shift in my life. And, the shift happened in one day after making my list! I never imagined how appreciating and loving myself would change everything. Focusing on loving myself brought the relationship of my dreams. I've never been in a relationship before where I felt so safe and appreciated. Susan you're a genius! In the last week, four different people, friends, a coworker and a family member told me that something about me was different, that I had a "different light about me." My mother said that she has never seen me so happy, that I finally appreciate myself and that you are the best thing that ever happened to me. Susan, you're on fire. *AL, Chicago, Illinois*

It's so comforting to me that I'll be talking with you soon. If I think back to the space I was in when I found you, how I found you, and how (seemingly) random my selection was of you off that list of coaches, I have to smile at how perfect it all turned out. You really are a blessing Susan. Omg, what if you're an angel or just a figment of my imagination?! Oh, wait, never mind. I've seen your FB posts. If you're real to other people then you're probably bona fide. *DA, New York, New York*

I wanted to share my experience with coaching with Susan Shearer Young. Because it helped me so much, I am betting it can do the same for others. Susan and I hit it off right away in the initial free session; it was like speaking with a friend I've known for years. I had a lot of different things going on—not feeling I was where I wanted to be in work, a relentless crush on a guy (heck, I was in love with him), a need for a better living situation, a book that just wouldn't write itself. By the end of our sessions, work wasn't perfect but I knew how to get myself into a better feeling place about it within a very short period of time. My apartment is much more comfortable and charming, and bad neighbors (and a bad building manager) manifested themselves right on out of my experience. I feel more patient with my writing process and have had the courage to show my prologue to a few trusted friends, which motivated me to keep going with it. The guy ..... well, things ultimately didn't work out with him, but **I got something **so much better**--a healthier attitude toward romantic love. I know what I will and will not accept, so some of the loser guys I tended to date (because I was frustrated at being single and not having** him) manifested out of my experience as well. **I no longer tolerate disrespect or people stepping all over my boundaries and am 100% happy being single until the right one comes along. Compared to where I was before (bad drinking problem, being mistreated by men, sporadic burst of crying, sleepless nights) – I'd say that's awesome!** For every negative thought or manifestation, she can find something positive about it to help you turn it around and, trust me, I presented her with some pretty grisly things. I feel so blessed to have met and worked with Susan. *HH, Los Angeles, CA*

You are an awesome coach. You are the first person who has taken the misophonia seriously and has looked for a solution for me. I think I told you that I had been avoiding Googling it because it would depress me and then I'd feel hopeless. You are also the first person that I've met that can and actually wants to hold a conversation about Abraham, our guides, and basically anything LOA. I initially thought that you would get on the phone each week and listen to me speak about all that I feel is wrong in my life. It was a welcome surprise to realize that you do a lot of work behind the scenes for our benefit before you get on the call. I am really striving to put your tips and suggestions into practice in my daily life. You are definitely a blessing and an anchor of peace. *AS, Scranton, PA*

What to say about Susan's coaching abilities. If you are just looking for a coach then you are so in the wrong place. She is more than a coach; she is a sweet, caring, loving, Divine being who is truly in contact with her Source. If you will come with the true intention of doing your work, then you cannot ask for a better friend, support, and yes coach. She is loving and caring and patient. So if you are ready to find yourself your Source and tap into it and WAKE UP to the power of who you really are and step into it, then she is your guide. With all the Universe's love, find YOU and know SOURCE HAS YOUR BACK!!!!! *WJ, South Lyon, Michigan*

Susan, I just wanted to tell you that you're right, I owe you a million dollars! This works. It really works. {Personal details omitted} is happening again this weekend and I'm totally okay. You know why? Because I KNOW it will work out. I know it. I have moments of doubting it but then I shift back into KNOWING it and it WORKS. Haha, all that talk about finding a better thought is true! I was just looking for a better thought in the wrong direction! I MEAN WHY DO I EVER DOUBT THIS LOA STUFF?!? I've been feeling moments of doubt today but DAMN. Wheeeeee!!!! IT WORKS FOR MONEY IT WORKS FOR RELATION-SHIPS TOO. You don't have to answer this but I wanted to say thank you, I already love you. *AC, Atlanta, Georgia*

Susan, I wanted to tell you how much I appreciate you, that you saved me. Things are completely different than when I started. I was going in the wrong direction and now things are completely different and better. I'm so much happier. It's really an honor to work with you. *RB, Asheville, N*

Thanks for all of your help. You have been integral to all of the changes I have been through in this last year. I write about my appreciation for having you in my life when I use the Daily Tool. Thank you a million times over. You are saving my life. *MK, New York, NY*

Working with Susan was an absolute joy! Each week she came prepared with great new ideas and insights for me to think about and use. She really helped me to clean up my vibration around sticky topics/situations. I made huge improvements in my belief system during my time with Susan, and manifested some wonderful opportunities along the way as well!! While working with Susan, I developed an awareness of where I was in relation to my vortex. Susan is very generous and kind and so easy to talk to. She is really perceptive and intuitive, and I can't mention how many times she would pinpoint exactly what was going on and tell me exactly what I needed to hear. I looked forward to our calls where we would get into the vortex and have fun creating what would come next. I highly recommend working with Susan. You will enjoy it and benefit! *SJ, New York, NY*

To find out more about coaching, Susan's coaching platform appears at www.howtoallow.net/coaching. Susan can also be reached at Susan@howtoallow.net

If you have benefitted from "How to Allow," I would be honored if you would review this book on Amazon.

Susan Shearer Young

Printed in Great Britain
by Amazon